INSIDE

Brian Greenaway knows prison life from experience. Chelmsford, Winchester, then four years in Dartmoor.

He knows how hard it is to stay human in 'the time machine'.

But something happened to Brian in prison that gave him hope. Nowadays he goes back inside voluntarily – to share this hope with today's cons.

This book, the sequel to the bestselling *Hell's Angel*, is both his story and others'.

Brian's story is told by Clive Langmead, a freelance writer and broadcaster for the BBC, and a former ship's navigating officer. Clive is also author of *Worse Things Happen at Sea*, a lighthearted account of life afloat.

INSIDE

BRIAN GREENAWAY
with Clive Langmead

A LION PAPERBACK
Oxford · Batavia · Sydney

Copyright © 1985 Brian Greenaway and Clive Langmead

Published by
Lion Publishing plc
Sandy Lane West, Littlemore, Oxford, England
ISBN 0 85648 842 9
Albatross Books Pty Ltd
PO Box 320, Sutherland, NSW 2232, Australia
ISBN 0 86760 658 8

First edition 1985
Reprinted 1989

Printed and bound in Great Britain by
Cox and Wyman, Reading

Contents

1

Hard Man

The door of the remand cell crashed open. Framed in the opening stood the court policeman. I looked up, setting my expression immediately into a mask of hate and loathing. The policeman sneered in return, determined to show that he wasn't afraid of me.

I laughed inside. Who was kidding who?

Everyone was afraid of Brian Greenaway.

Twice convicted on violent charges, now up for a third stretch. This time the sheet read 'malicious and unlawful wounding'. And I'd meant to kill.

My Angels had been out on a bundle – Hell's Angels that is. Some soft kids had been messing on our territory. Messed up one of my mates too, so he said. As President I didn't need much encouragement to go out and thump them.

They weren't for real – all mopeds and plastic jackets, that kind of rubbish. They were just asking for a short, sharp piece of education from the genuine article. We'd soon shown 'em who was a Hell's Angel and who wasn't.

Only they weren't quite so soft when we ran into them in down-town Gosport. I'd had to do some damage. In fact, dropping acid, I'd freaked out on the spot and couldn't quite remember what I'd done, except that I had upheld my reputation — for hurting hard. But I soon discovered it had been a set-up. My so-called mate had grassed.

Just after we had got back from our little party the Old Bill had rolled up mob-handed — four big coppers. I wasn't about to argue with them. I went quietly.

Down at the station as they leaned on me it came out that mine was the only face that had been identified. Fifty guys in a bundle and my face the only one to be clocked. Pull the other one. Tony had fingered me, turned Queen's Evidence, that much was clear.

I hoped the Queen would make it nice for him. He'd need all the help he could get when I came out.

"Time for the beak, Greenaway," grinned the copper.

It was time to face the Judge for the last time — for him to pass sentence.

I saw my guard had brought his mate with him in case I was going to cause trouble. Well, I always liked long odds and would hate to disappoint them. Eyeing him evilly I lunged up quickly off the old wooden bench that served as a bed and made as if to go for him. Psyching him up. He recoiled instinctively, cannoning into his supporter behind.

I pulled back. The grin broke out onto my face, though it was nothing but a twisted leer. I never had intended to do anything, anyway.

So much for hard coppers.

But however much the guardians of the law might flinch when Brian Greenaway jumped, the Law itself did not. As I was led for the last time through the narrow basement corridor to the Winchester Crown Courtroom, I felt an unfamiliar stab of fear.

It was time for the reckoning. I had admitted my guilt and was due for the punishment.

At first I'd pleaded not guilty, naturally. But with my mate standing next to me shooting off his mouth at every opportunity, my chances of convincing anybody that I was mummy's boy had begun to look a trifle slim. On my defence lawyer's advice I'd changed my plea. He said it would help me to get a short sentence.

How much I'd be weighed off for I didn't know – though I hoped it would be a few months, like before. Anyway, a bit of bird was a doddle. Piece of cake.

I entered the courtroom. Once again I was struck by the stage management of it all. It was like a play on TV. The judge in his great robe and ridiculous bobbed wig; the prosecuting and defence lawyers with their black coats and lifted noses. How different was all this gear from the garb I had worn as President of The Nomads? None that I could see. There was the same absolute authority, embedded in clothes and lifestyle, except now it was power over me, not mine to use as I wished. My future was in someone else's hands now, not my own. It choked me off to think about it.

And, what was more, I knew they didn't care.

I could see it in their eyes, in the way they talked to each other in hushed whispers, looking round at the courtroom, at the ornate woodwork, the delicately carved chairs, the inlaid painted ceiling – anywhere but at me. Excepting perhaps the odd glance of unholy fascination. I was just another job to them. An item on the legal agenda, somewhere between rape and burglary – something to be disposed of. It just blew my mind.

I shuffled up to the dock and took up the pose I had

adopted over weeks of appearing in the court: a studied and arrogant slouch. I gazed insolently at the judge, through half-closed eyes.

First off – three months back – I'd stood upright, answering the questions as quickly and politely as I could. Then, as the weeks rolled by, I twigged them. They just weren't interested. Well then, neither was I – and I showed it. Every week, as I was brought before the magistrate, I would amble in, kick the dock door open with a crash (that woke 'em up) and slouch on the rail, slurring my replies, begrudging every straight answer. Real co-operative like.

They wouldn't forget me; I made sure of that.

"Greenaway – remanded for seven days," was all I ever heard, polite or indifferent. I felt better being the latter.

Cool, hard and angry was the way I liked to play it. It made no difference anyway.

But now it was for the last time.

"Greenaway!" The beak was talking. I cocked a sullen eye. He fixed me with a gaze holding all the sternness he could muster – aiming at an impartial judgment. But the distaste in his voice was ill-concealed.

"You are little more than an animal, Greenaway – someone who enjoys filth and dirt and who considers violence normal, not hesitating to resort to it on any pretext, disturbing and endangering peaceful citizens in the lawful course of their daily lives. Not only that, but you have taken it upon yourself to lead others, more gullible perhaps, down the same unnatural paths. . ."

He paused, sensing his words were making little impact. He continued with almost a sigh.

"You will go to prison for four years."

He might have added 'for all the good it will do you',

but he didn't, and anyway I wasn't listening, just reacting.

Four years!

It had come out so suddenly that I nearly jerked with surprise. I held my cool − barely.

Four years. Well, I'd been told it might be. I'd had fair warning from my defence lawyer, if no one else. Even though I had changed my plea to 'guilty' at the last I still had a lousy record. But four years was pretty stiff going all the same.

A wiser man might have reflected that it was lucky the charge hadn't been murder − and the sentence 'life'. But my victims had lived (not something that I'd intended at the time) and I'd got weighed off for 'just' four years.

I tell you, it was as good as life to me.

All I had ever wanted was to be free. Free to ride around where I wished, leading my chapter from the little youth centre in Leigh Park, just outside Pompey (Portsmouth). Going where I wanted, when I wanted. Flashing through the country lanes of Hampshire on my mean machine − my gleaming bike − to the roar and throb of the hot exhaust, high on drugs, low on cares, pulling the birds, ruling the roost.

With no job and no home to speak of, physical freedom was the only thing I'd had left. Now it was gone. Not for three, six, nine months, a year even. But four years.

Four changings of the seasons, four Christmases (just sentiment, to me with no beliefs, but it still mattered). Four hot summers − or would they be cold and wet? I wouldn't know or care, thanks to the beak, the wigs and the robes. A brick wall is the same in any season.

Now there'd be no more grassy roadsides to lie on, no open sky to gaze up at and shape clouds in, no green trees to lean against, no soft girls to hold, no good mates to race the open roads with. Just a load of old cons, stone walls and steel – hard, black steel – and clanging, rattling doors shut in my face.

And, of course, the screws.

The Old Bill was bad enough, but at least their power ended when the charges had been laid at the police station. By then they had done their worst. It was in the hands of the court after that.

But in prison – even on remand – there were the screws, the Prison Officers. An army of sergeant-majors, whose every whim was an immediate command, every petty dreamed-up regulation law – at least for the con.

These were the people I hated more than anything. Little tin gods they were. *The* enemy. Now I had to live under them for four years. Was I beginning to lose my cool?

2

THE ENTRY PROCESS

The prospect of many years in prison has hit me like a ton of bricks...
    Letter to Brian from him, HMP Brixton, remand.

Quickly I was hustled out of the dock. No one wanted me to break out in curses and violent behaviour, as they all knew I might. But I stayed cool. It took some effort but I needed to make that impression.

All the time though, I was just steaming away inside.

My six mates, including 'helpful' Tony, were left behind to face the beak. They had been standing along with me in the dock – very carefully to one side out of consideration for the part they'd played in stitching up their leader. I was obviously being shown out fast so as not to hear their, much lighter, sentences.

Nothing like a little shopping to lighten your porridge.

Only this one had been cashed in on my ticket. It made me feel real proud to be their leader and president. On remand I had turned over again and again how they could have all come out so much against me. They all knew I would come to get them when I got out, however long. And they had chosen me as president; I thought they still respected me. I'd never stood them up. What was worse was that they'd set me up when I was out to avenge Tony, beaten at the hands of another mob.

I never let on but I was cut deep by their turning on me. It felt like the final betrayal.

I didn't know it then, but I was to find out later that another Man had experienced betrayal by his friends, in an even more bitter way, that ended in death.

The truth was I had got more and more crazy and unpredictable over the past months: dropping LSD acid tabs most of the time, taking bigger and bigger risks with chapter, straining the good relationships I'd had going.

I'd been told a while back that I was almost a head case. During a previous stretch in Chelmsford the prison psychiatrist had told me I was a psychopath with suicidal tendencies. An accident going somewhere to happen. Now the chapter had begun to see it too, and didn't want to be part of the crash when it came.

Many of them were drugged and hopeless like me. But they didn't have my bitter hate, my scorching terror of nothingness, my vicious obsession that the world owed me a living and should be made to pay. They just wanted bikes, booze and birds, with hard drugs thrown in – excepting perhaps Pete the Animal, my lieutenant. He was half on my wavelength, but even he had tired of my style by the end.

Pushed too far, and leaned on by the law, they had cut me adrift on the sea of my own troubles. All they'd done really was to give me a little shove off – the rest was of my own making, as my 'form' showed.

"It could hardly be worse," my defence counsel had said, looking at my record. It seemed that the beak had agreed with his assessment, and had made his judgment accordingly.

The policeman hauled me down from the dock, swung me through a couple of doors and snapped on the handcuffs.

"Want a blanket?" one of them asked quickly. I couldn't angle his meaning and looked stupid.

"The Press, laddie, the Press. Cons like you" – he savoured the word heavily – "get attention. Can't think why."

I refused his offer, which had in fact been a kind one, with a snarl. I would milk my moment of glory for all I could get. They could put my name up in lights for all I cared. In fact I was hoping they would. Just now I needed an ego-trip like a cold junkie needs a fix. I wanted something to pick me up off the floor. Being the centre of attention just fitted the bill. A hero at last; I'd made the papers.

Outside the court the reporters were waiting. It gave me a real kick to know that I was a notorious criminal now. But my slice of fame went stale. I was allowed only few seconds to stop and talk and all I remember was a girl with a notebook – one of the reporters – a beautiful blonde girl, a real looker. Bravely she came up to me and asked me some questions. I don't know what I said, but I couldn't forget her, her freshness, her style, her eager confidence. She spoke hauntingly to me of freedom, shouting out at me what I had lost. A final parting slap in the face from the outside world. I remembered her for days and weeks afterwards.

The drive from the courthouse to the prison was a short one, straight up the High Street in Winchester. The Black Maria laboured heavily, its engine wheezing, as it made the grade. I didn't see the heavy iron-studded oak gates swing open to allow us through, as the windows of the van were shut and barred. But I heard the familiar jangle of the keys at the screw's waist as he checked the driver's clipboard and clanged open the inner steel grid.

That was the flavour of prison. Keys and checks. That and boiled cabbage in the kitchens.

With the other convicted prisoners − we were all cons now − I was escorted to a featureless room with high windows, to await processing for formal entry into the prison system.

Although I had been an inmate for three months already, it had been only as a 'remand' prisoner. Unconvicted, innocent until proved guilty, I had been allowed to keep my own clothes and personal things, given full use of any money I had and one or two other freedoms. It wasn't much, but at least I wasn't a con. In theory at least I was still a free man. Strange though it might seem − for I was still locked up for most of the day − this last was actually a great comfort. And this despite conditions in the remand wing being frequently much worse than the rest of the prison. Take the ceiling of the reception room − it was covered with impacted blobs of margarine thrown up by bored and fed-up prisoners. No one had ever made the men clear up the mess. Remand was unpleasant, but you weren't a con.

Now everything had changed. I'd been weighed off good and proper. From now on I was doing bird.

Along the wall of the 'welcome' room stood a number of wooden cubicles − like a row of open toilets, except with only a bench inside. One of us was ordered into each 'horsebox' and there we waited, banged up, with a wire grill to peer out of until they came back for us.

Today we were lucky. It was already late and the processing work started almost at once. Sometimes new cons have to wait the whole day round before the system catches up.

Three screws came in. One of them seated himself at the battered desk, another stood the other side and read our names out from a clipboard, the third attended the horseboxes with his keys. As the names came up, the owners were brought out and pushed forward. Some were nervous and still shocked, some old and worn-out, some confident, grinning with bravado.

My turn came.

"Greenaway!"

The 'Mr' had been lost a long time back, but there was an imperious tone now to the call. No lawyer would be lending me an ear for a long time. As a con they could push me around with impunity. I got to my feet, as leisurely as I could but not sullenly any more. The screws were just waiting for aggro, ready right away to stamp on any problems − literally.

From now on I would have to steer a careful course. On the one hand I wasn't about to cause myself any more trouble (unless I could get away with it). But on the other I was someone special. I needed my self-esteem.

"Yes, boss?" I responded, avoiding the usual − and demeaning − 'sir'. I had no respect for screws.

"What you in for, Greenaway?" he barked, his mouth two inches from my ear. He knew perfectly well; the screw at the desk had my papers in front of him. The question was not for their benefit, but to make me state my crime out loud in front of the others.

In my case there was nothing to fear − perhaps something even to gain. My crime was respectable in the strange hierarchy of prison − I'd only tried to kill someone. Quite worthy really, and perfectly acceptable. But if I had been a sex case, a 'nonce' −

child-molester or rapist perhaps – then I would have started sweating. I might try whispering my offence to the noisy interrogator warming my ear, but it would do no good. He would continue to ask until I shouted it at the top of my voice, for all to hear. Then, inexplicably, all the screws would suddenly find the need to leave the room. "Just for a moment, lads – be good, won't you".

The screams of the helpless offender would be lost in the noise and bustle of the prison as the waiting cons left their cubicles for a few violent moments to vent their own anger. They had mothers, daughters, children of their own. A 'nonce' had it coming, and usually got it – hard. I kicked one down a flight of steel steps once, when I was in Exeter. He just happened to be handy.

I was stripped down naked in front of the screws and my clothes flung over a screen behind, my tattoos showing up colourfully against my pale white skin. Already I was taking on a prison pallor from three months on remand, sort of greasy yellow. A trustee – a Red Band, onto a good number here in the reception room – went quickly through my pockets, piling up my trinkets, cash, whatever, on the desk. The screw noted them all on a form and sealed them, with my clothes, in a plastic bag with my name and number attached. They would be returned, with the list to show nothing was missing, at the end of my stay at Her Majesty's pleasure.

As he was doing this, he fumbled and somehow my small packet of tobacco – 'snout', the main currency of prison – slipped carelessly out onto the lino. My bag was sealed up and I was marched off to the bathrooms.

As I left the room I heard the red band exclaim, "Oh, look, sir! This must have fallen out of someone's pocket, I can't think whose it might be."

The tone would have done credit to Shirley Temple.

It fooled no one. The screw glanced up and said nothing. The snout disappeared quickly into the man's pocket. I did my best to remember his face. But Winchester is a big prison – and I was naked.

I went on through to the 'sheep dip', or bathtub rooms. As I scrubbed off, another con wandered in and asked my size for uniform. The bath space was open and anyone could just walk in. I growled at him to get out. It was shameful to have him gazing at me, assessing my build, in the bath. Quite likely he was a fairy anyway and had volunteered for the job. I wasn't about to give him any ideas. He shrugged and left me. I got out, dried myself, the strange prison soap leaving my skin rough and flaky, and joined the queue for clothes.

I was then issued with the only type of clothing I would wear for the duration of my sentence: blue-and-grey-striped cotton shirt and bib-and-brace overalls. There was also a sort of coarse 'suit' of grey, hairy flannel, which we used for best – seeing visitors and such like. That had to last your time. The shirts and overalls were replaced as they wore through – if you knew the right people. I also got a pair of black, round-toed shoes. I tried them on last. The fairy had got his own back: they were two sizes too large, and the clothing hatch was closed.

Boots, of course, would last much longer but they are good for kicking – and I don't mean footballs – so they are not issued. They think of everything; you are allowed to think of nothing. The whole thing was, and is meant to be, a humiliating experience. Stripping you down in front of others, shouting at you continually, taking advantage of natural shame and fear of the unknown.

Identity is shattered on purpose. Conformity for easy handling is the requirement.

Prisoners have few rights (none that can be exercised without an appeal to higher authority), and must always do what they are told. They may speak only at certain times, must be silent when ordered and ask permission to perform even the most basic of human functions. Any slip and they know that this can cause them 'loss of remission': more time behind bars.

The entry process is a sharp reminder of all of this. But many never manage to beat it. I've known cons in for a three-year stretch still in after five. Just couldn't handle it, themselves.

An animal? Maybe the beak hadn't been far adrift.

I'd always known the score, but that made the game no easier. And this time it was all going to take very, very much longer.

101 – Living Under the Shadow

99 – Let your living water

45 – Great is The Lord

189 – You are beautiful

29 – Exalt The Lord

100 – Lift up your head

3

WINCHESTER

All through life from about the age of eleven I have always been against authority, especially police and courts. I have always been the one who thought I could take care of myself ... I had to fight my way to where I wanted to be ...

Stuart, HMP Strangeways, life

Winchester Prison was nothing new to me. I'd done a lot of bird there before.

My first stretch had been at Winchester. I'd had three months at a detention centre as a kid but later I'd scored a year for violence. The first part of that had been here. Firstly this was because it was local to my home, such as that was. But secondly Winchester was an allocation prison: where men are kept and watched and judged before being told where they will spend the rest of their sentence. Now, with the others, I was waiting to be allocated again. The waiting can take up to a year.

It was an unsettling place with so many on the move. Like many of England's prisons, it was a Victorian building left to grow out-of-date in the twentieth century.

Except that prisons can't grow. Their walls are fixed. Winchester held roughly three times its original intended number, but the seams weren't splitting – the sardines just got packed a little tighter.

Living together three up in a six-by-twelve-foot room may be OK if you've got somewhere else to go. But banged up in a peter most of the time with screws breathing down your neck – well, I can tell you, some of us enjoyed it so much we never stopped laughing. Most of those are psycho cases, now allocated to Broadmoor, where they are assured of a secure, long-term future.

Winchester also had a Mailbag Room. Though every prison has its 'workshop', somehow mailbags seem to stand out as an occupation in my memory of Winchester. Yep, even today cons still sew mailbags.

The bag shop consisted of a set of benches standing in parallel rows in a long, low room. Each of us was issued with a thick needle, thread, tar-like beeswax and a roll of canvas (or hessian) sacking. Only one needle, mind you, and carefully accounted for – a sacking needle heated and pushed backwards into the plastic handle of a toothbrush makes a very handy little 'persuader' when it comes to debt collecting round the landings.

We were then told off to the benches eight at a time, and ordered to sew. Nine stitches to the inch, no more no less. The rules say we don't rap to anyone except in our own row, and we don't stop for nothing except the sound of the last trump.

In with the needle, up, back and through; in, up, back and through, a crusty pad of work leather on the ball of your thumb to force it out – four-and-a-quarter hours every day. (The clock used to take its time in the bag room, too.)

One stitch wrong – the standard depended on the screw in charge – and you did it all again.

There was also a quota to get done, set by the fastest. Get a flash kid who'd learned sewing at his mother's knee and all the rest of us had to try and keep up – at least until we'd had a quiet word with him, in a quiet corner. A bunch of fives would quickly help him put his whole contribution in perspective. The pace would ease from then on.

Something that put *our* contribution into perspective was the machining room next door. There one man with the aid of a sewing-machine could produce as many bags in an hour as two rows of us in a day. Such vital work we had on our hands, and we knew it. . .

We got paid — 84p a week. We also got holes in the thumb. You could always tell a bag worker: little black marks all over his thumb and palm, where the needle had slipped and stabbed, mixing beeswax with blood.

But it wasn't the pain I minded. Just the monotony. Apart from the work the bag room brought the art of verbal communication down to the level of a teddy boys picnic. And hark who's complaining.

Talk in prison tends to narrow down to two things: justice, which has never been done — at least according to the speaker — and getting 'on the out' somehow or other, legal or illegal. Fantasy runs high on both fronts, and so do feelings. Successful appeals, great escapes, powerful friends — all are thrown about in deluded hope. Knock backs (failure to get parole), petitions to the Home Secretary (the right of any prisoner who feels he has a grievance), and intentions once outside (mostly illegal and, as in my case, vengeful) form a rather more realistic and entirely monotonous dirge of conversation strung together with continuous profanity. Not that I minded that — then — but there is a pathetic whining tone to it, which gets to you after a while. Actual success is rare. The system makes sure of that. But talk is cheap. Someone might be impressed, one day. So the rabbit goes on, along with the sewing.

But before I faced again the delights of the bag room there was the reception line. On the first morning came the visit to the governor.

"Greenaway stand up!"

The screw was already standing in my peter. I hauled myself off my bunk, protesting. He indicated the door, and through it the stairs down. Then, without a word, alternately leading and following he escorted me outside across to the admin wing, unlocking and locking the gates and doors in endless succession before and behind me. His heavy boots clanged on the hard concrete, his keys jangled at his waist. Out we went, across tarmac exercise yard, the cons walking steadily round and round in concentric circles; the hard ones, the top cons (barons) in the middle, the lightweight nothings at the rim. And always anticlockwise, never any other way.

The door to the admin block was the only one so far that wasn't locked. Inside stood a group of other prisoners under the guard of one screw. The two officers nodded to each other and I was left standing with the group, but my escort didn't leave. I realized then that I must be under consideration as a category 'A' prisoner — a designation reserved for only the most violent and dangerous of men. Men who could be relied upon to do very little that was sane, being just about as vicious and bestial as it was possible to be.

If so I would have to have a guard at all times when moving about the prison, usually with a dog as well. I could go nowhere at all without surveillance and could be banged up at any time and kept without warning if conditions demanded it. Needless to say my inflated and warped ego took this possibility as a compliment.

We entered the governor's office. Two burly screws stood between me and the front of his desk. They faced towards me, their features unmoving. I was rammed up against them by my mentor, facing the governor. He was visible over two strong shoulders and framed by two unmoving ears. Evidently nobody was taking any chances. He looked up from his brief perusal of my file without expression. He made nothing of the occasion.

"Number 278431, Greenaway, your Earliest Date of Release is. . ." He read out a date from a card.

I didn't take any notice. Three or four years from now would be the time to start worrying when my bird was up. A date way off in the future makes no sense at all. Later I did worry. I remember getting an exercise book and ruling it off – a square for every day I would be inside. It became my countdown to freedom. Nine hundred days, including remission, if I behaved. In fact most cons have some way of keeping the tally.

I was spun about. My interview with the governor over. No one had mentioned a category. Next came the Chaplain.

Chaplains come in two styles: direct and dippy. Some are Christians, some aren't. Some love the bottle, bed and breakfast, others have hearts as big as mountains, will turn out any day or night if you need them and carry godliness around with them like a warm cloak. I didn't know which the chaplain at Winchester was, and at that time I wasn't interested.

"If there is anything I can do . . ." he was saying. The usual claptrap. Verging on the dippy.

"Forget it, Vicar," I snarled. "Unless you can get me some acid."

He smiled tiredly. He had heard it all before. Drugs had been easy enough to come by in the remand wing; I'd had money there. Now it was going to be a bit more difficult. Cold turkey beckoned. Acid was on my mind.

He smiled as well as he could at the lout who

confronted him.

"Are you asking for hospitalization?" he queried. No, he was direct.

"No mate." I could take turkey if I had to — it wasn't too bad coming off acid. Or maybe I could become a drug baron and support my trips on others' needs. I'd done it before with tobacco, no sweat. There was sure to be a network operating inside which I could hook up with.

"All right, Greenaway, that's all."

Short and sweet. That was just the way I liked it.

Next came the doctor. This was going to be a thorough examination if past experience was anything to go by.

"Cough, Greenaway,"

I coughed. Standing naked in front of the man, with a screw one pace behind, I couldn't do anything else.

"Fine, any problems?"

Only a few I could name. He eyed my tattooed body with distaste. A lot of people did that. It gave me a kick. But he was concerned about the medical implications — at least I think so. He said nothing.

"Next."

I was fit and well. High-quality, the prison health service.

Last on the list came the welfare officer. Sort of chaplain without the neck-gear plus probation contacts on the out. A probation officer on secondment, his job was to assure me that my family, such as it was, would be kept informed of my situation and that there would be work and accommodation for me when I eventually got free. To tell me, in fact, that once my bird was done, all would be sweetness and light.

Some of us believe in fairy stories.

I held my bottle with this one. He said nothing about

the out, nothing about home and family. He looked at me, tapping my file.

"Not a brilliant start is it?"

His voice was level, not kindly, not accusing. It was just a statement of fact. I knew well enough what he was talking about — and it wasn't my bird.

I'd had a spot of bother on remand, you see. Actually I'd freaked out — really far out — with two screws who had tried to do me in my cell. I had been making waves by overheating on the call-bell for a cell-mate with toothache. Nobody was coming and the man was in agony. I had just leaned on that bell button. Soon the other cells were ringing too. It was great fun, helping the Hells Angels wind up the screws (there were eighteen in on remand at the time, from different chapters, though I was the only president). Well, they'd come eventually and the dentist got his patient — and I got a couple of incensed screws in my peter. They came for me and I gave as good as I got. I've said I liked long odds.

The screws didn't like it. Loss of face, plus bruises. They'd given me a turn in the 'pigsty' for that — a filthy cell set down below the others in the block.

But the final straw, it seemed, had come last night. First night in as a con. I'd been banged up with a new cell-mate.

"What's your stretch?" I asked.

"Two weeks," he smiled. I blew out every gasket.

"What the . . . *get him out of my cell!*" I screamed down the length of the block.

"*Two weeks!*" I would kill him. Petrified, he hung on the call-bell, begging for mercy, not knowing what he'd said or done wrong.

The screws had rushed in and dragged him out before I murdered him there and then. His belongings quickly followed, helped by my oversize shoe.

There was I with four years stretching ahead of me and they had put me in with a man doing only two weeks.

The welfare officer was frank: "It doesn't look good."

I asked him what he meant. He said he couldn't say; it wasn't in his province. We completed the formalities and I left, uncertain. What had been meant? Was it perhaps a kindly warning to expect bad news? Or just another threat? Category 'A'? That must be it.

I was soon to know. The following day the deputy governor's round revealed all. I was called in to the defaulter's room at the bottom of the block. I stood at attention at the end of the T-shaped table, the longer section projecting into my stomach, a screw on either side. He was a long way off, safe from my reach, but his words carried quite clearly.

It seemed that, after all, I too would have only a fortnight to serve in Winchester. . .

"Greenaway, number 278431." He instigated the proceedings formally without preliminaries.

"It has been found necessary to transfer you urgently, without the normal allocation time. Frankly there was no need. We know what you are like. Winchester is not a suitable establishment for men such as yourself."

I gloated inside. They were on the run — getting rid of me. He looked down at the movement order in front of him, as if to convey the official nature of the opinion it contained.

"You will be moved to HMP Dartmoor at the next transfer."

A cold blade of fear slid into my stomach. The screws at my side moved slightly, reacting to the news in their own way, offering a little unconscious sympathy.

"Yes sir," was all I could find to say.

4

THE MOOR

The weather is still very cold, it did try to snow today but it stopped, I am always glad to get into bed on nights like this. . .

David, HMP Dartmoor, life

Hauling up slowly out of Winchester in the early morning, the prison bus headed west on the Dorchester road, dipping and lurching across the undulating landscape I had conquered so often from the bucking saddle of my bike. Handcuffed to a screw, nose up against a barred and breath-hazed window, I could do little but peer fitfully out onto the chilly winter scene and dream of past travels, blanking out the uncomfortable future.

At each prison town we drew briefly to a halt to deliver some luckier inmate into the arms of his new home.

Exeter was the last of these. A prison I knew well – I'd done most of my last bird there. Not half bad, as prisons go. I'd made it good then – as a tobacco baron, loaning out my snout, a quarter or an eighth of an ounce at a time, for double the amount back. The standard rate. I built up quite a 'bank' of it in the end, farmed out to 'keepers', of course, the prison regulations only permitting a man to carry two ounces on him at any one time.

I was big enough and mean enough to do the collecting — always strictly on time. But after a while I'd got fed up smashing weedy villains in the mouth when they couldn't return the goods. Being a baron was no big wheel really. Happy times though, I thought.

As we climbed up the first of the foothills the change of the countryside — from frosty green vales to rocky moorland, granite spikes pushing up through the sparse brown bracken — spoke of the bleaker future ahead. The future I didn't want to face.

I checked around the bus. From an original full load we were down to eight. Only two cons, one of them me, the rest screws. The Moor was to be the end of the road.

The silence was, well, thoughtful as the toiling vehicle mounted the first of the tors and dipped, shuddering, into the valley beyond. The grey free-stone walls on either side of the road seemed to act like rails to its progress, forcing us onwards and upwards into the misty and now darkening heights of the moor. A capsule of warm humanity in a desolate and hostile waste. Maybe, I thought, I would be destined to ride this road forever. Boring ever onward through the gathering gloom, crossing peak after peak, plunging down valleys, crossing black, racing torrents, twisting round perilous bends, grimly looking out between the bars for the lights of my destination — which would never appear.

We'd become the 'flying dutchman' of the moor, damned to travel it for eternity.

I certainly felt damned and lost. My brain was fantasizing — out of fear probably, or maybe the acid was catching up with me.

Once or twice I caught what I thought were

sympathetic glances from the screws. They weren't too thrilled about being appointed to Dartmoor themselves. Princetown, the village adjacent to and dependent on the prison, wasn't exactly vibrating with city life. Nor for that matter was it full of cheery west-country rural charm. It was a dormitory for the prison staff, little more. But they also knew what it was like in the wings. They knew the sort of friends I would have to make, the regime I would have to endure. After all they were running it.

There was a certain sympathy.

It was funny, back in Winchester when word had got out, I'd had a few 'knocks on my door', some even from screws.

"Shame about the Moor, Greenaway," they'd said, some with a hint of triumph in their voices, but nearly always mingled with a sense of pity.

"The Moor?" I'd reply. "Can do the Moor standing on my head."

They might have been impressed — which was the idea — but I wasn't. I was downright scared.

Her Majesty's Prison Dartmoor was built to house the French prisoners of war in the days of Nelson. Built by them, for them; to release them from the overcrowded prison hulks, then anchored in Plymouth Sound. It had been run at first by the Navy whose brutal traditions seemed to set their seal on the future. Later the (newly-formed) prison service took over. The harsh regime remained, although prisoners of war were replaced by criminals and cons. Terrible were the stories told of the old days at the Moor. Hundreds had died within its walls down the years. It was old, monolithic, forbidding. And so remote was it that it had now become England's maximum-security prison for violent offenders. A pool of the vice-ridden and vicious.

The ultimate antisocials. The bent, the barbaric and the broken. Most of the inmates were there for violent crimes, some were killers, a good many were in for life – 'lifers' who had nothing to lose by being just as downright difficult as they chose. The rest were so far gone that the screws would almost keep their peters aired for them when their bird was up; they knew they'd be back again within weeks.

Recently I'd taken a liking to reading cheap westerns. In one of them a group of hardened prospectors had decided, cynically, to name their shanty township, No Hope City.

Got it in one. Dartmoor could have been their home from home.

The coach climbed higher and the mists began to blanket the view. As the early January darkness became night we entered Princetown, home for most of the screws. Some of them got out. My escort, handcuffed to me, stayed.

Granite is a hard stone. Most of the houses were made from it. So was the prison which loomed suddenly out of the mist, gaunt and fearful, lit up by the anti-personnel lighting which shot watery green arc-gas beams into every corner of the compound within the gates, and onto the perimeter walls. We drove through the heavy, iron-studded gates, entered the courtyard and were surrounded – by granite. The weight of it fell on me and I felt crushed. It reared up all around me, in walls, in buildings, underfoot. My spirits sank to the very depths.

Suddenly, instead of it being a great place for tough cons, a place I feared but was determined to crack, the prison seemed a place of intense sadness, a collector of shattered human lives, of broken spirits, tormented hearts, outcast minds.

As we drew up a working party marched by. The end of the day. One of the cons looked up at me, and with a contorted laugh pointed me out to the others who jeered and shook their fists. There was madness in his voice and gesture.

I wanted to spring from the bus and kill him, jump on him, tear him to pieces. Through the mist of my anger I caught sight of my face in the window of the bus. My face, my expression, was the same as his.

The next day the welcome routine was run through once again. I saw the governor over the shoulders of some screws, grunted briefly at the cleric and coughed heavily at the doctor.

But it was with the welfare officer that I lost my bottle. I was marched into his office to be greeted with a friendly smile.

"Hello, Greenaway." He offered me no seat, it wasn't the practice, but I could see the thought was there.

"Well now, Greenaway, what are we going to find for you to do when you get out, eh?"

I stared at him. He'd made a bad blunder. The fool thought I was just about to leave.

"No, I've just got here," I explained thinly.

"I know that." He smiled again. "But we do have to think of the future sometime, you know."

I freaked out.

"*Future!! Getting out!?* I've only just got in and you're talking about getting out!?"

I panted heavily at the effort of physical control to

stop myself leaping across the room and smashing him there and then, and with one blow probably doubling my sentence. My head was spinning wildly.

The welfare officer was shocked. He had met violent prisoners before – often – but not such a violent reaction to what had seemed to him a normal conversation. His job after all was to find me home, work and acceptance outside the walls when my sentence was over.

But I had been there before.

In the past, whether due to the overloaded system or to failure on the part of others, I had found their promises hollow, their assurances void, offers of a job scheme and a room of my own outside, non-existent. After my last stretch I'd been promised a welcome in Portsmouth Probation Office, and a helping hand. I had turned up. They'd never even heard of me! Con-merchants of the first order they were, all of them. As far as I was concerned, they'd led me round in circles, and got me back inside.

It made me angry.

"One more word – and you're dead, mister," I hissed. And I meant it. I'd have got him somehow.

Wisely he kept quiet. He could see I was in no mood to discuss anything – long-term or short. Raging I was led away, back to my single cell – which latter was about the only advantage there was in coming to the Moor. A single peter. Mine. I could at least be alone with my anger.

I didn't know then that I had just seen forged, under very strange circumstances, a vital link in the chain that God had decided to hook onto my life in the Moor – to drag me into the future that he had in mind. At the time all my self-pity permitted me was hatred: at yet another of the insincere, taunting mini-gods of the prison system set up to make my life just that little bit more unpleasant if they possibly could.

As the weeks rolled by, I found that another mini-god whom I had served was also turning against me: LSD. There wasn't much around and what there was I couldn't afford. I'd been dropping acid on and off, mainly on, for over five years now. I'd first been given it in Chelmsford nick. I found it helped soften the deal that life dealt out. I sometimes used to take it to wind me up for a fight, though, unlike some, I never needed it to build up my bottle.

It just helped me relax at the youth club, or just plain let me forget. In prison if you could get enough snout, you could get some acid by doing a deal — it was easy enough to smuggle in, contained in tiny microdots. Virtually undetectable. But I hadn't the bread.

I knew about cold turkey from the day of my conviction, along with one or two of my mates. I could hear them screaming and sweating at nights, around the wing. The screws were used to it and didn't interfere — unless one was so bad he needed the doctor. Acid doesn't have the hold that heroin and some others do. In a sense it is easier to kick. But that is only relative. Kicking it was hard — and LSD gives you flashbacks, for years after. It triggers your mind, unexpectedly and unaccountably, and there is nothing you can do about it. You could be up a ladder, driving along the road, cooking a meal, and suddenly you are back ten years before, the present gone, the past all round you — sights, smells, distorted memories everywhere. You have no control until it passes. You could kill yourself. Some have.

Even when I got out I had a long process of drug

rehabilitation to go through — at a centre. But the worst of it was that now, inside, there was no soft cotton wool to help me escape the harsh reality of life as a con banged up in the Moor.

Every move was uncushioned: there was no escape anymore, not even inwards.

5

LAW OF THE JUNGLE

Once I decided that friendship was a sign of weakness.

Gary, HMP Wakefield, ten years

The thin winter daylight had not yet penetrated the cross-barred window of my cell when the slight scraping noise of the flap opening on the 'Judas-hole' in the cell door told me that it was seven a.m.

An eye winked briefly in the opening and then the flap slid closed.

The screw moved on.

A minute or so later, muffled by the thick steel door, I could hear him report the head count:

"Landing D5 – twenty-three present, sir!"

On the stone-flagged floor below, the principal officer in charge of the wing scratched at his clipboard, tallying up his list as the count was shouted down from each level.

"Correct. Next!" The dawn chorus continued.

At last the final number was indicated and checked off.

All present. Nobody had done a runner overnight.

"Right, unlock!" came the order. Quickly the screws

worked back along the line of cells twisting the key in the door with one hand and slamming it back with the other.

"Slop out!" they roared.

Yawning and cursing at his untimely enthusiasm I rolled out of my bunk and staggered towards the bucket in the corner – my toilet in case of need during the hours of darkness. I felt awful. In a daze I grabbed the handle and turned towards the door to join the others now spilling out onto the landings en route for the 'recess' or tap room. The screw, who intended to make sure that this part of the day on his landing went smoothly, put his arm across the door, car-park barrier style. Through the mists of sleep I heard him wisecrack, "Not forgotten anything have we?"

I cursed roundly, before remembering that I needed my water jug as well as my bucket.

A running tap of hot water would be streaming away in the washroom and all of us had to line up for washing and shaving water after ditching the contents of our buckets. We took the water back to our peters to wash. Well, I couldn't very well use the bucket could I?

Forcing myself awake, I took down the metal jug. The screw dropped his arm, letting me through.

I can't cope with mornings.

I staggered along the landing to join the others, sluicing my bucket out and filling my jug. Next to the recess there were a couple of proper toilets.

I didn't bother with them. For starters they were open to the view and inspection of all who joined the water queue. That sort of thing freaked me out. I could wait.

If you were a nonce or owed snout you had to watch the morning queue. A jug full of near-boiling water over your head, followed by the jug itself in your face, was a normal way of quietly being reminded how things stood. The gang of men in the queue or huddled round the tap would prevent the screw spotting the trouble until the damage was done.

Or maybe a razor blade slipped in your bar of soap, so you could carve yourself up when you beat it back to your peter.

Razor blades were issued very carefully to prevent this kind of thing, of course. After slopping out the screw would come round with his canvas pouch. In it was a blade for each con, wrapped and slid in a slot with the cell number painted on it. He gave it out just for shaving, and in twenty minutes you gave it back again. You had only the one and there was no chance of anyone getting any more. Or was there?

One way was to give back a piece of card carefully wrapped like a blade, hoping the screw wouldn't check it properly. With hundreds going in and out the chances were you'd get away with it. The blade was then yours for the day. Something to even the odds a little in a disagreement. Or razor a nonce.

But if you were caught, then it was a serious offence and loss of remission would follow.

Loss of remission is the standard punishment — meaning more bird. With any sentence one-third is automatically 'remitted' — taken off — on entry. From this is calculated your EDR: Earliest Date of Release. Any bad behaviour — breaking the rules, annoying the screws, breathing without permission and so on — and days' or weeks' 'loss of remission' would be added to your time. This could continue, at the discretion of the governor, until the whole of your original sentence was dropped back on top of you. If you still bucked the system he could then wheel in a tame magistrate to weigh you off some more — on the evidence of the screws, of course.

Next it was time for breakfast. Shaved and washed, we appeared once again at the shout and clattered down the landing stairs tooled up with our knives and forks.

We were all issued with a knife, fork and spoon on joining, along with a mug – all plastic, mind, so we couldn't stick anyone – and that was ours for the duration. They did OK. It was as much as some of us could do to handle a knife and fork anyhow. It really is the dumbest types that end up doing bird. Like me.

You know, I found out later that ninety-eight per cent of closed-prison inmates are working-class, like me again. Fact.

The food was served on trays. Right on the tray. No plates. The steel trays had dents and scoops in them for the various swill served up. Not having too many seven-course dinners three dents was enough, plus a round hole for your mug.

We were never short of bread – for any meal. You could grab as much as you liked. Marge and something to go with it came a little thinner – one pat each. You made it go round about five slices, and all the food got put in sandwiches too. Pasty face? Sure thing, but a guy has to eat.

For breakfast there was usually something else as well. Porridge. You could almost have handed it out in slices like the bread.

There was also a burnt offering: rubber eggs were a favourite, beans were popular too – no, not with us – they weren't baked beans; these were dry, white ones. Must have been a job lot going cheap, back round the turn of the century. And tea to drink that I swear was sold outside as weed-killer. To this day I still cannot drink a cup of tea. As they say: the flavour comes flooding back.

At a quarter to nine we were let out. Freedom! No. Circles in the exercise yard. That was if it wasn't raining. During exercise was the time to go to the toilet. There was one nearby which had a door. There was always a queue.

Following exercise round the yard – fenced off from the wall by fifteen yards of perimeter patrolled by dogs – we reported for work.

At the Moor it was no longer mailbags. No, up here they were sophisticated: I was sent to the television shop.

This was a real step into the twentieth century. We were assembling television sets. Wow, some step, eh? Electronics wizard in two weeks. Stroll on. All we did was put coloured wires into coloured holes. You know: red wires go into red holes, green wires into green holes and blue wires into blue holes. I tell you the pressure was really on. Sometimes a set needed *two* wires put into each hole.

You had to take a break to ease your mind after tackling one of those.

But on the whole, although the screws were stricter and the eyeballing closer, the Moor got liveable after a while. Of course the faces were different. Gone were my old Hells Angel mates who had been picked up with me (and grateful too, I guessed) and gone too were the screws I'd come to know and love in my time on probation.

In that nick I was known as a hard man and president of a chapter, and that reputation had followed me down. I made sure it stuck. Most of the deal in any nick is showing that you've got the bottle to lean on anyone who has it coming, and aren't about to let anyone get lippy. You get respect. If you don't everyone will start putting you down, trying it on. The harder con you are the better you get on. Simple law of the jungle.

Take an instance: in the lunch queue, if you don't get a decent portion you stop until you do. They tried it on me just a day or so in, but only once. . .

The piece of fish was small, and shrivelled, and burnt.

"Hey, mate, what do you call this?" I challenged the con doling out the food over the heated steel servery.

"Move on, mate," he said distractedly, deliberately doling out a portion to the man behind.

I held my ground and swore, loudly. "I said I want another piece of fish!"

He turned, apparently seeing me for the first time, grabbed my tray, slopped off the old piece and replaced it with another, even worse. The sauce ran all over the top.

"There you are, mate."

I looked at the tray which he was holding out to me, then at him. I narrowed my eyes. My fist came up to waist level as I bunched the muscle. Across my knuckles was tattooed the word HATE. Grabbing the slippery tray I rammed it down onto the servery. His hand was underneath. It connected with the hotplate.

"I want another piece of fish," I repeated slowly, my eyes searing into his. His began to water, ever so slightly.

"Oh, ah, my mistake, mate." The tray was returned with a full portion.

The law of the jungle. Look after number one and stamp on the rest. It was the only way. Most of us there were animals anyway. Of about 300 cons, 120 or so were gutless and completely prisonized, total members of the institution who had no hope of making it on the outside. Many of them were never going to get out anyway.

The rest were the worst sort, hard cons (including me), all violent, with histories of horror and deprivation even I found difficult to hoist in. They lived in a private hell of their own as often as not. Wound up about their past, guilt-ridden or brazen by turns, resentful of any help or interference. I was all of that.

But it was the nonces that always got dealt the worst hand. Even if they wanted to they could befriend nobody.

Not long after I joined I met The Beast. An ugly brute of a man inside for molesting children. He liked to play table tennis during the evening association, when all the cons were allowed to mix freely in the two hours before being banged up for the night. I fancied my chances at the game myself. I couldn't stand watching TV. The screws would always turn it off (with a grin) at about ten to nine − just before the climax of a film or whatever. Something like that bottled me up too quick. Ping-pong was a fair alternative.

The Beast was good and seemed to enjoy the friendship as well as the game as he lumbered around batting the ball skilfully back and forth, easily catching my amateur swipes. I could see I would need to get in some practice before I had any chance of beating him. Well, I had all the time in the world for that. But after the game a screw fingered me on the landing.

"Watch it," was all he said.

I took no notice. Some screws were paranoid about GBH cons − had to keep the lid on, tight. I just thought he was leaning on me.

The next night I played again. This time the screw was waiting for me in my peter when lock-up time came.

"Do you know who you are playing with?" he asked. "That's The Beast."

"So?" That was no staggering revelation.

"You be careful. You go on like that and you're going to get your card marked."

I began to get the picture. The Beast was too strong to be 'given a physical'. So they'd decided to get at him another way. No wonder he was so pleased to have someone challenge him to table tennis.

And I couldn't afford to have my card marked. After my little run in with the screws at Winchester the last thing I wanted was to get a name for annoying them at the Moor as well. I could wave goodbye to any remission if that started happening.

I grunted some reply, trying to blank it, but I had no choice. The word had been put about: No one plays games with The Beast, talks to The Beast, helps The Beast out. The Beast doesn't exist. His crime was being alive at all.

I made other friends.

Oddly too I made a sort of friend amongst the screws. Doug came from Portsmouth — and that was home. Occasionally he used to chat about the old town. He was probably as lonely as me stuck up there in the prison officers' quarters at Princetown. He wore long sideburns, like they did in Pompey at the time. It was enough that he would talk to me, about places and pubs we knew. I didn't get any visitors so it was my only link with something familiar, a reminder of the real world. We could even call him 'Mr Jameson' sometimes, rather than 'sir' or 'boss' as expected. But memories were all we could share. A con gets called 'iffey' if he chats to screws too much. Can't tell what he's stirring up; screws can turn so many ways.

The best screw was Arthur Rodd. The man was his name. Straight as a die, firm, no nonsense. If you messed up he dropped on you like one of the great granite flagstones in the courtyard. But if you had a case, a problem, he would see to it, hear you out – and not forget to do something about it. You knew where you stood. There was no familiarity, but also no hassle, no favours, no nods and winks. A man amongst animals.

But I still hated the system, as a con all of it was against me – and the screws were part of it. It burnt on deep down in my innards. There was nothing that was ever going to change that. As winter turned into spring and spring into summer, my tortured mind wound tighter and tighter in on itself. The granite walls grew closer about me. I knew now that things could never change.

As it turned out I didn't know much.

6

SUNDAY

I do hope when I come out. . . I can change. I don't want to go back to my old ways of drink and drugs. . . I'm going to church every week now. . .
Bill, HMP Wandsworth, five years

It was Sunday morning.

As everyone knows Sunday is a day of rest, so, as usual, we were all banged up in our peters, resting. After slopping out, breakfast and exercise, a normal day would find us manufacturing more TV sets in the 'box shop' – or, as I was now seconded to the Works Department (building and maintenance) party, doing a bit of painting and plastering, running electric cables or pointing up some brickwork.

Not on Sundays. Back we went to our peters and clunk went the door. Banged up for the day.

There was one exception: church. At about half-ten a screw would shout: "*Church and chapel!* Time to dust off your Sunday best."

We all roared with laughter at that one. After all, he said it every week.

Those of us who wanted to go would then indicate by pressing our bells. The tell-tale flap then fell down outside indicating religious interest. Those who had done this were unlocked and shepherded into three groups according to the coloured 'inmate' cards outside each cell: C of E, Catholic and The Rest. The Rest ended up as Methodist.

Quite a lot of cons went to church. Some out of tradition, most out of boredom. Sunday was always so long. I decided to join them – as a Methodist. Well, the C of E chaplain was a thoroughly nasty piece of work at the time – a screws' man – and I couldn't call myself a Catholic, so that kind of reduced the options.

I went along just to see some of my mates really – from the other wings. There was little chance otherwise and I could put up with the singing and the rest of the service just to see another face to relate to.

There was also one other bonus – they gave away a free newspaper: the *Methodist Recorder*. You got one of your own. Not like the daily papers in the wing, which you had to queue up to read – and never got your hands on. This was yours to keep. I used to read it from cover to cover. I mean, I could give you the running style of the Methodist Church month by month better than the President of Conference himself.

To me it was just information – could have been the *Ferret Fanciers' Gazette* for all I cared. Excepting on the back page there was an advertisement for a Yellow Bible. It was just a picture and some chat, nothing wild, but next to the picture was a bit of the text, printed out to show how it read – and I could understand it!

That was news. You see, I had come across Bibles before. Back in Winchester, on remand, we used to have a penguin come and visit us, regular – me and Pete the Animal.

She was an older nun, a real gentle lady, used to come about once a week. Knocking on the door she'd slip quietly in with a smile, springing the lock carefully so she could leave quickly if she had to. Sister Bridget.

Without turning a hair at the sight of us, she would sit down on the bunk and ask how things were, how we felt. Had we heard from our friends, our family, maybe?

Occasionally she talked about God. Not much, because that used to wind us up.

"Over there – he's my god," said Pete, pointing across the cell to me. Half the time I think he really meant it.

Then she would look at us, grave and gentle, trying not to show how hurt she was. She would leave. She had others to see.

We respected her and never cursed or clowned about when she was there. She, in her turn, never condemned us or pointed a finger. I could see she was trying to love us, but I didn't know why, or what it meant, and took no notice. It wasn't for me. I wasn't a God-botherer.

We were high on acid most of the time there anyway. Part of us wasn't in the prison at all.

After she'd gone I used to pick up the Gideon's Bible for a laugh – the old 'Authorized Version' (there was one in every cell) – and read passages out loud to Pete.

Up and down I'd pace, booming out the thees and thous, waving my arms and foaming at the mouth like I'd seen American preachers do on TV. Pete would cower in the corner when I got really going, screaming at me to stop, especially if I was on acid. He knew then I'd be close to freaking out and I guess he didn't know what might happen.

After a while I'd quieten down and throw the Bible aside. What a load of outdated old nonsense.

And now, on the back of the *Methodist Recorder*, there was a whole paragraph of the Bible I could understand. It was written in the clearest of English – and the words all made sense!

I wanted one of those Yellow Bibles. I didn't know why, but I did.

Apart from Sister Bridget I had only ever had respect for one other person to do with the church. He was Peter Hancock – Reverend Peter Hancock.

I'd met him first when I was in the process of taking over his youth club in Leigh Park – for my Hell's Angels.

I'd found the club just after it had been built – and decided what a nice headquarters it would make for the chapter. We moved on in. We were heavy into youth work, of a kind. Working youths over, more like.

I didn't know that the centre had been built from the funds raised by several churches in the Portsmouth area. Not that it would have mattered. Churches were full of rich spongers and hypocrites as far as I could see, anyway. It was about time they gave something back.

Peter's church was one of them. Well, of course, when we fetched up at the club and made it our home it didn't exactly begin attracting the sort of young people the churches had been thinking about, so one day a couple of brace of vicars showed up, to check the place out – three dog-collars and an open-neck shirt. The open-neck shirt belonged to Peter.

We made like we were innocent of all the nasty things people had been saying about us and hung around batting ping-pong balls at the ceiling, while they snooped about.

There was nothing they could do. We weren't breaking the law – or the club – and we weren't so old. Real fine young people, with a deep interest in motorbike mechanics. They just had to congratulate themselves on the good use to which their fine building was being put. Trouble was – most of our bike-chains tended not to be used for driving bikes.

But while they were making 'tsk, tsk' noises under their breath, and trying to think of ways of making us move on, Peter really seemed to take an interest. In his relaxed gear he wasn't so obviously a vicar of the stuffy establishment. He could see we were young people trying to say 'help'. We had needs − we just covered them up.

He wasn't busy trying to stop himself throwing up at our greasy leathers and our acid-head manners. He could see a mask and wanted to know what was behind it.

From that first, rough, meeting (we'd eventually sent them packing with some verbal you'd look hard for in the Bible) he went on trying to get through to me. Praying − and stopping round from time to time.

Soon after I got put away for the first time, Peter visited me inside. Drove across special all the way from Portsmouth to Lewes just to see me. I was jack the lad then − big and cocky − and I don't know I showed much gratitude. But I felt at least he was trying to get to me as a person.

What's more, when I got out he met me and drove me round and round Leigh Park looking for a room to rent − and then he paid for the first week. That cut a lot of ice. But I was too heavy into the drug scene and keen to get back on my bike.

How did I thank him?

Occupied his youth club all over again.

But for me, church in the nick was really there just so as I could meet my mates. I had made a few over the six months or so I'd been up in the Moor.

There was Shaker Roberts. He was a pimp from Southampton. Not my line of country really but he was a bit of a mouther, and could keep my humour up. He was also a 'tasty guy' – someone who was hard and mean, and not all just front and rabbit. He was good to have around – he and me: twice the safety. We also had a nice plan going. We'd always laughed at the security of the low outside wall of the Moor. Compared with some it was nothing. Fifteen maybe twenty feet at the most. With a bit of planning we could easily do a runner. Every day on the exercise or in the workshop or at church, we would plan for the day that we were going to get over that wall. Of course we didn't know anything about the camera system, the miles of open country, the trained Escape Response Team – and all the other sophisticated items that form part of the cage that keeps you in. We thought that once we were out over the wall we'd be away. We were bound to make it.

I had taken some instruction from an ex-paratrooper in my block who had told me all about fieldcraft, making hideouts in the open, setting up booby traps for hunters, to put them – and their dogs – off the trail, or in hospital. He also taught me how to handle explosives, how to fire guns properly, how to maim and how to kill. Right little finishing school he was running. He wasn't the only one either. There was Ace, from D wing, too: he taught how to crack safes. Tinker Seb from Cell Block 3: nothing he didn't know, or wouldn't share for snout, about smuggling things in and out of the country.

I shared all this with Shaker. One day we would do the runner.

One day.

Then there was Chas. Chas was an 'Angel' from Wolverhampton. Now chapters and chapters aren't supposed to mix. Not on friendly terms anyways. Some do get together, but pull someone's bird, or turn your face the wrong way and you can forget the brotherhood of the road. Count it nice going if you can get away with your skin intact.

Not inside. Unless the blood is really boiling hot between chapters, Angels have something in common. It was bikes and old times in the saddle that gave us something to talk about.

And he was just my type. We were looking at the same length of bird together – four years, less with remission. He was also a tasty guy – in for GBH among other things. We decided that if I didn't go on the trot with Shaker we would wait our bird out and then form a team.

We had a neat idea. We'd take bikes round the country and aim to hold up late-night petrol stations with shooters, sawn offs probably, taking the cash. If anyone called our bluff we'd let him have it in the legs with both barrels. It seemed a cool way of earning a few bob. Yes, Chas was going to be a great help when my bird was up.

These were the sort of people I was going to church to meet. I looked forward to it – anyway it was safer than association time when you never knew who was going to have a go at you for something. Always tense, association. At church you had time to relax just a little.

This morning I was in for a bit of a surprise. The minister, Ivor Earle, asked me to read the lesson. Well, I noticed it was open at the Book of Revelation, whoever he was, and the place was marked up. I stumbled through with it, messing it up all over, but the reverend seemed satisfied and I had managed to get a few smirks out of the twenty or so lads who'd come along. Bit of a laugh. Trouble was he asked me again next week. I was getting to be a right little expert.

We worked slowly through the Book of Revelation. It was strange and weird, all about the end of the world. But one line kept coming up again and again and began to stick in my head. I could almost feel it coming as I read the verses: "Those who have ears, let them hear!"

I wondered, was someone trying to tell me something?

7

YELLOW BIBLE

I feel I have come to the end of the road. . . I have started reading the Bible but it just seems like it is a book just full of writing. . .
Simon, HMP Exeter, twelve months

In the Moor I never had any visitors.

I can't say I had too many in previous prisons, either, but there was usually someone who would come round sooner or later.

Not in the Moor. You had to be someone real special to get people fighting their way across Dartmoor to see you. It was a long way from home.

Once two of my mates did try to come down and see me on their bikes − not long after I'd been transferred. I was still fresh on their minds. The only problem being they decided to liven up the ride by stopping off at most of the pubs on the way down from Pompey to Princetown. Then, as a chaser to the beer, they dropped a tab or two of acid.

By the time they burned up to the main gate of the nick they were tripping out wild and in no mood to take on the formalities required for visiting a maximum-security prison.

They were happy enough to take on the screws though.

Fortunately I knew nothing about this, being banged up. Only when the governor called me up to his office did I realize what I'd missed. He sharply informed me that I *would* have had a visit if the 'friends' in question had not decided to punch ten kinds of stuffing out of the officers on duty at the gate. It made me sick at heart.

Naturally the screws had turned my friends round smartish and told them none too gently to forget any idea of getting in to see me.

Blown out of their minds though they were, they took the hint and hared off back the way they'd come. They were lucky the screws didn't put the Old Bill on their tails.

Of course there was nothing I could do or say. But if there is one thing that is worse than not getting a visit, it's expecting one (the visit forms have to be completed beforehand) and then finding it all sour up on you. I could have kicked their faces in myself for screwing it up the way they had.

So, as I say, I was kind of thin on visitors.

Then, around August time, Terry Scarborough – the welfare officer – wandered into my peter. He was the one I had gone off at when I was doing the welcome routine on moving in. It had taken him six months to get over my aggressive behaviour, but he had – and he came in with smiles all over. Like a cat that's been at the cream. I couldn't make him out.

"How would you like a visitor, Brian?" he asked.

Well, you don't just go in feet first at suggestions like that. Someone could be winding you up. So I replied even-handed, like, "Might".

Inside I was really stirred up. A visitor! But I was wary after the last failure – and anyway what would

Terry have to do with any of my visitors?

He took my reply as encouragement to go on.

"Well there is this farmer, lives round abouts — his son is really into bikes. He works in a garage, fixing them up. I figured you might have something in common with him, Brian."

By now I was really firing on all cylinders. This was good news.

"What's he want to see me for — eh?" I swore for good measure.

"Just a chat, that's all. I'll see if I can fix it — if you're interested."

He looked doubtful for a moment.

"Could be."

Hey, I was nearly brushing my hair and shaving my face, getting ready.

He went ahead and made the arrangements.

A few days later I got a visit-notification card: 'Mr Malcolm Goodman has been given permission to visit Greenaway 278431 on Friday 15 August'.

Then the week went by in a rush of anticipation. I must have been a model prisoner. By the time Friday came round I was like a teenager on his first date.

When the time came I was shown into a room in the education block — not one of the usual visitors' rooms, with glass and a hatch, but an ordinary room with a table, and a chair either side. I sat down. After a few minutes a screw came in with this older man in tow, who almost looked as nervous and excited as I was. It turned out it was his first visit to the prison and I was the first man that he had been allowed to see. I don't know to this day why I was chosen to get the visit but there we were, two strangers sitting together in prison, with a table in between us. One of us a near-killer and a confirmed psycho head-case (I had actually been visiting the prison psychoanalyst for some weeks), the other one a gentleman farmer who wanted to visit prisoners.

We talked, slowly at first, but then, as he explained his son's business in custom bikes — he knew a bit about it himself — I began to warm towards the man. He seemed a decent sort. We chatted for about half an hour and then the screw indicated my time was up. Malcolm reached out his hand. I took it carefully. It had been years since anyone had offered me that sort of friendship.

"Anything I can get you?" he asked, innocently.

My mind flashed over all the things I would like — trying to work out how I could get him to smuggle me in some tobacco, perhaps, or some...

"What about a book?" he added hurriedly, remembering what he'd been told by the governor before coming in.

Suddenly I remembered the Yellow Bible I'd seen on the back of the *Methodist Recorder*. I wondered if a man like him ever went to church. Would he even know what I meant?

Uncertainly I stumbled: "Would you know a thing called the *Living Bible*? It's sort of new and has a yellow cover and I've seen it in this ad on the back of the ..."

I stopped, held by the look of amazement in his eyes. Without a word he bent down and opened his case, which had rested forgotten on the floor during our conversation. His hand came out with two books. One was a yellow book. On the cover were the words LIVING BIBLE. He turned and gave the books to the screw.

It was my twenty-seventh birthday.

The next day the books came to my cell, having been checked by the censor. He had to look through any gifts, including books, to see that there was nothing hidden inside and that they were suitable reading for cons. I hoped the *Living Bible* had passed quickly.

I looked at the cover of the other book. It was called *Run Baby Run* by Nicky Cruz. But what excited me most was the sharp stiletto that filled most of the cover. This was going to be good: a story of violence and terror, a story set in the streets of New York where teenage gangs roamed and fought. It had to be tops. The blurb on the front said it was supposed to be true as well. I knew about gang rumbles and chain fights and the like. More than most, I guessed, I would know if the story was true or not.

I began to read. It was half past four in the afternoon. I missed tea. The summer sun was glancing red-gold bars into the cell when I first looked up from the page. My heart was pounding.

A deep and perilous fear had crept across me.

I was reading about myself. The names had been changed: the scene had been set in America. But it was my story. True from start to finish.

Nicky had been a gang president. Vicious, bitter, trapped in a cycle of his own madness. He was afraid of nothing except himself — and what he might do. Not even afraid of death. In fact he often set himself out front in fights almost hoping to be killed — except he was too good at fighting, too thorough at hurting with flick-knife and zip-gun.

It was *me*.

But there was another part of the story. Nicky had run across a spindly little back-street preacher — who had gone into the slums of New York to speak to the gangs, the pimps and the winos. But especially the gangs. The preacher had talked about God, about forgiveness, about love — something Nicky had never known —

about Jesus who loved so much he was killed for it by jealous men, but whose death had made it possible for everyone to be accepted by God.

He had found out that Jesus Christ had died for him, would forgive and accept him if only he would admit his own need. His self-centredness, his sin, had to be named before a just and mighty Creator, whose love for him had never come to an end. God really was there, said David Wilkerson. Waiting.

And, after a terrible struggle, for the first time in his life Nicky had surrendered.

I put down the book and found that I was sweating and shaking. My hand trembled. My eyes did not want to focus anymore, pricking with tears. I felt I should stay very still. Without knowing quite what I was doing I picked up the Yellow Bible, my fingers fumbling and searching for a page, any page. I let it fall open where it wanted to and began to read. It was a chapter from John's Gospel:

'I am the true Vine, and my Father is the Gardener. He lops off every branch that doesn't produce. . . Take care to live in me, and let me live in you. . . I have loved you even as the Father has loved me. Live within my love.'

Suddenly, in the stillness I felt a Great Presence surrounding me and pouring into me. I felt a surge of love ripping into me, tearing away all the layers of filth and dirt, boring down to my heart, dissolving the hate and the bitterness, swallowing up my tortured self-centredness. A blast of joy rushed through me, clearing me out like a great vacuum cleaner. All my sinister passions, lusts and sick longings drained away. I was filled with a peace and a joy that I'd never known, and couldn't understand.

It was the rushing Spirit of Christ himself. Round about me was the harshness of the cell, the steel of the door, the granite of the walls, the solid iron bunk. He was as real as all of these and yet I saw nothing, heard nothing, felt nothing — except inside. But the power was there. I had never before been so overjoyed — and so afraid. Like Nicky I had never known the meaning of surrender, until then.

It was another birthday. I knew I'd been born all over again.

There was a turning of the key in the lock and the flat of a hand on the door. It was time for association. I got up and walked unsteadily out of my cell. Shaker, the pimp, was on the landing.

"Shaker," I whispered, shaking all over but feeling wonderfully at peace and calm.

He looked up from lighting his roll-up fag, surprised at my tone.

"Yes, mate?"

"Shaker, something's happened. Something very strange. I don't know how but. . . I. . . I've just become a Christian."

8

THE SCEPTICS

Brian, I just didn't understand, and it still takes an awful lot of believing. Put it down to ignorance if you like. I thought that you were just working your ticket...

Chas, HMP St Loyes, three years

It was about a week before the taunting started.

Disbelief at my belief had begun almost immediately. Some, like Shaker, showed shock and contempt at my new conviction, but, knowing me as a person, kept up the bond of friendship. Others blanked me straight away and scarcely spoke again. Nearly all showed by their looks that, whatever sort of experience I'd been through, it could do me no harm in front of the Parole Board.

"Working your ticket, eh, Brian? Don't worry, we'll not squeal to the screws."

I would try and explain. "No mate, look, Jesus Christ came into my life – for real, man. Just took me over. No con... honest."

"Yeah, yeah, we twig it, Brian, no need to lay it on."

"No, look mate, something really happened. Jesus..."

The language would more than likely hot up and I would find that unless I wanted a fight on my hands I would have to back off with my explanations.

Then the taunting started. I don't remember who it was – and at first I was quite pleased in a backhanded kind of way. At least if they were taunting then it meant that they took me seriously.

"Hey, Brian, had any Angels hanging round your peter recently?"

"What about heavenly voices, Brian? God bent your ear much lately?"

"Any chance of a light, Brian? No, don't get up – just sling us over your halo for a sec."

All of sudden, Brian Greenaway getting religion had become flavour of the month.

But what was most incredible during those first few days was that, although I did really mind, I did nothing about it.

After coming to the Moor I had put myself about a bit and kept up my reputation as a hard case. No one got lippy. Now, sharpened up by their mates, even the wimps in the nick were having a go at me. Never having said anything more than 'sir' for the last five years they would suddenly find the courage to come up and laugh in my face, crack a Jesus joke, or just push me out of the way on the landings. Days before they would have ended up with a broken skull – for starters. Now I had to stand back and let them through.

But I knew God was there. He meant everything to me. The status I had earned in the nick, the petty jealousies, the need to be on top of the pile or get crushed at the bottom, all of it had evaporated in the pouring, raging torrent that had swept over me. Its warm, comforting presence seemed to stir inside me wherever I went.

But things were to get harder. I hadn't counted on being liable for a physical. But one guy had got himself wound up about something. I don't know what it was.

He wasn't the verbal type.

He caught me in the washroom.

"You the Jesus-freak?"

I had to admit that I love Jesus.

Wham! Right in the teeth. Blood spattered across his knuckles from my broken lip.

"Got to turn the other cheek then, haven't you?"

For a moment I was stunned, not by the blow, but by the whole deal. I would kill him. My bottle was up and I was on the verge of freaking out. He could see it, alarm spread across his face. But God was there. Suddenly I relaxed. I dabbed my bleeding face with the arm of my shirt and turned away.

Seeing this he pushed past me, elbowing me aside, confident he had shown me who was boss, one more rung up the jungle ladder, over the head of a Hell's Angels president. Except that he was ignorant of the power-struggle in heaven and in my heart. The power struggle of love.

For I knew that was what it was. My experience had been powerful, life-changing. No question of that. But life-changing experiences are not that rare. You hear about them every day in the newspapers, if you look. People are always getting to crisis-points – and having experiences which change them totally: a car smash, birth of a child, holiday of a lifetime to a strange land, death of a close friend. Shattering, life-changing.

But mine wasn't like that. It was a simple experience of love. Nothing else. I knew that whoever had come into me and taken me over was both powerful and loving. The spirit of Jesus Christ himself.

Slowly, day by day, I discovered as I read my yellow *Living Bible* that what had happened to me was also nothing unusual or strange. All the followers of Jesus Christ had experienced his outpouring of love right from the early days. We don't hear about it so much today because most of the modern churches are more interested in religion than faith. In fact it was the keen religious types who had Jesus killed. He messed up their idea of the sort of people God would accept: sinners, whores, loan-sharks – Hells Angels. First off the church was full of them. Jesus had come to save, really save, my sort of person. He was there and he did it. That was what love was all about – taking on board someone who deserved nothing, less than nothing, because he loved them no matter what they had done.

Knowing that was worth a smack in the teeth – anytime. Now it was up to me to show that same love to others, maybe help them get right with God themselves.

But, filled as I might have been with the love of Christ for everyone, within three months I nearly killed a screw.

He was called Mercer. I never knew his first name. He wasn't the sort. In fact I hadn't seen much of him around the nick until I started talking about Jesus.

Well, that seemed to really turn him off – in a big way.

He made it his business to watch me every hour of the day that he could spare. He would pick me up on all the little jobs I'd missed out on. At slopping out he would suddenly appear from nowhere and point out a corner of my peter that wasn't quite straight, or a footmark on the floor – probably where he'd stood himself a moment earlier. Patiently, without complaint, I had to stoop down and clean it up.

Sometimes the provocation was so great I would glare up at him, my eyes flashing, before the love of God took over again.

That was just what he was waiting for.

He would put his face up close to mine, breathing out at me, his finger prodding my chest.

"Call yourself a Christian, Greenaway? You're nothing but a spaced-out acid head who's lost his bottle. Eh? You don't fool me." He would prod my chest in time with the words.

I could only rock on my heels, the familiar violent war going on inside. The strength of God battling the pressure of my old self – and the prison rules. One move in the screw's direction and a tidy slice of my remission would disappear into the Dartmoor fog. It was almost understandable that my mates, or those of them who still cared to be involved with a Jesus-freak, would take the trouble to test me out with jeers and taunts from time to time. It looked very much to them that I was doing my best to get early parole and subsequent release – working my ticket. But from the screws – the guardians of the law in prison. That was hard to take. Instead of being grateful that they had a reformed character on their hands, they seemed to resent it.

Especially Mr Mercer.

It was as the nights were drawing in again and the cold winter wind was sweeping bitterly across the moorland, buffeting and whistling round the granite towers and blocks of the prison, that things, very nearly, came to a tragic head.

One late afternoon we had just been let out to go down and get our tea. I queued down with the others to get my pile of bread, square of marge and dolop of jam and carefully made my way back up to my peter.

On the way I passed Mr Mercer. Unusually he didn't look at me or make any comment and continued his measured tread down the length of the wing.

At the top of the steps stood Doug, the screw from Pompey.

"Evening, Mr Jameson," I muttered casually as I made my way along the steel landing to my cell door.

As I turned the corner I felt a blast of cold night air. Odd. I hadn't left the ventilation window open, I thought. I glanced across to where my pet budgie fluttered in his little cage — the only friend I could count on and care for in the nick.

With a leap of my heart I saw that the cage door was open — in fact had been hooked back, as though I'd wanted the bird to fly out and flutter around the walls. When I'd left it had been tightly, safely closed. Now the bird wasn't there.

Without pausing my eye swept round to the source of the draft I had noticed. The ventilation grille in the cell window between the bars was open, wide open. It too had been closed when I had left for tea.

I let out a roar of anguish. My little bird, my tiny, defenceless bird. Someone who chattered and sang and took titbits from my hand, who fluttered against my cheek, who was warm and harmless in this prison of vice. She had been let out into the dark cold night to die on the moor.

With a violent surge of anger I knew who had done it. Mercer's averted gaze had said everything. It told me all I needed to know.

I freaked out.

With a snarl I burst out onto the landing and swung round. There would be one dead screw in the block tonight just as sure as Brian Greenaway lived. I would smash him into the ground. Mercer was at the extreme end of the landing. He had his stick out ready. But I was beyond caring. I roared with rage and anger. Screaming out his name I made for the bridge. Suddenly a hand went around my throat, another expertly twisted my flailing arms behind my back. It was Doug, alerted by the animal shout I'd made when I'd discovered the bird missing.

We wrestled awkwardly on the landing. I was kicking and crying, "He's got my bird, he's let my bird out, *he's killed my bird!*"

And Doug was shouting in my ear, "Easy man, take it easy. *Take it easy, will you!*"

To start with the cons, seeing the screw in trouble, had backed off, but when they could see I wasn't high on acid but freaking out over something important, they ran up and helped me — to stay just where I was. They knew that if I were allowed to go free there would be a lot to answer for in the morning.

Slowly I sank to the ground. Doug relaxed his grip only a little in case I was faking. But I wasn't. The blind anger had gone. He walked me back to my cell and sat down to talk for a few minutes, explaining that there was nothing he could do and that getting violent was not going to bring the bird back. I could get another one.

I nodded dumbly and stared sightless across the cell as he tactfully closed up the cage, the ventilator and finally the cell door — banging me up, gently, for the rest of the evening in case I got fresh ideas. With one last eye to the Judas-hole, a clink, and he was gone.

I stared at the wall for a long time, until like a huge kid I curled up on my bunk and wept, bitterly and silently, for the little life that had been taken away.

9

CARE AND MAINTENANCE

'I was in prison and you came to me' – are words that say it all for me and will stay with me all the days of my life. As a Christian I ask for your help as the road in front is long and full of problems. . .
Danny, HMP Wandsworth, twenty-one months

Living by the light of my new-found faith wasn't all taunting and set-backs. There was one thing I'd learned from my past life, apart from what to avoid, and that was to come up fighting – not now with chains and knives, or even (in the nick) with knuckles or a blade, but just fighting to 'carry on' as a Christian.

I read more and more of my Bible and I soon enrolled in a Bible course – doing all the study through the mail, getting my work (mostly badly-spelt essays) marked and sent back to me at the Moor.

The reason my spelling was all to pieces was not so much a missed education, though that didn't help. It was just that all the paperback westerns I'd read in my time made it look as though I was writing up my work in the OK Corral, not banged up in the Moor. Gave it all a sort of country-and-western flavour.

But faithful old Mrs Wilmer from the Methodist Study Centre alternately reined me in and spurred me on as, month by month, my letter arrived. The red lines slashed through the cowboy talk and naive comments, gently pointing out the truth and clarity of the Bible.

She told me nothing of her own opinions, urging me to look and think for myself − which was pretty hard at times. And she would pin her comments not on special lines − or her own favourite verses − but on the whole chapters, and how the themes related backwards and forwards through all the books of the Bible, tying it together.

And slowly a whole new, and very wonderful, world opened up which I had never dreamed of.

Of course individual verses and texts did matter − to me a great deal, considering the power those few lines from John's Gospel had unleashed in my direction only months before. But I also discovered they could be taken out, and bent, and wrongly used. The devil can always quote from the Bible.

It was just like using a bike repair manual (we used to call them our 'bibles' in the Angels). If you aim on stripping down a gearbox, you get nowhere at speed without all of the repair book.

Tried it once, using a mate's old manual. Couldn't afford the bread for a new one. Missing pages ripped out, greasy black finger-marks where he'd worked down it himself. Lines, whole diagrams sometimes, blotted out.

No problem. Jack-the-lad Greenaway could fill in the gaps. I knew the main bits. Wasn't much I didn't know about my Mean Machine.

After half an hour things didn't look so good. I thought I knew where I was going. After about an hour I didn't know if it was a gearbox I was working on or a true-life impression of a bombed-out ball-bearing factory. Cogs, springs, bearings, rods and bars all over the park. Probably would have offered me two grand for it at the Tate – on artistic merit alone. No good for the bike though. That was off the road for two weeks.

I went out and coughed up for a brand new manual in the end, with nothing missing or smudged out – and read it right through.

Then I got it right.

But back in my Bible – my real Bible – all I was reading confirmed not only what had happened to me that August in my cell, but also that I must expect opposition.

No matter what I did, Satan – and, as I was finding out, he was as real and as hateful as Jesus was loving – would be out to try and stop me.

There was nothing he wouldn't do to destroy my faith and if he could use friends, respectable people, my private hopes and fears, he would.

But Jesus was always there. It was up to me to turn to him – and to go on fighting: praying, trusting, hanging on, growing, understanding. Winning through with Jesus Christ.

I also started shooting back, when I could.

Nobody, but nobody, missed out getting a gospel message, one way or the other. Talk about a Bible-bashing. Mine was a Bible *broadside*. Anyone who hove into view caught the full effect: texts, convictions, condemnations, explanations – and, by God's grace, love too. At least I hope so, for in God's kingdom I was still so very young and inexperienced – all mouth and movement, not a lot of care and prayer. But I was going to try.

The first 'captive' subject for my endless preaching was Trevor. Trevor was a screw – but with a difference. He was a maintenance officer. This meant that his duties were (except in the case of emergency or riot) to supervise the cons in their various jobs of repair or building work round the nick.

I had just completed a three-month building course and on the strength of it I was appointed out of the hated TV shop to the maintenance party. I could have ended up mixing cement. As it happened I was assigned to work with Trevor, alone, on electrical maintenance. He was a decent enough sort. A slight lad, no older than me and real made-up that he was working with the ex-president of a Hell's Angels chapter.

That was until Jesus joined the team. After that he began to wonder which angels I was supporting.

I made sure he wasn't long left in any doubt.

First off, though, I was sent up the tall, swaying pylons to change the big glass-globe arc-gas bulbs in the prison anti-personnel lighting. I would go up the ladder and be able to gaze out over the low wall to the open moor and dream of the freedom I longed for.

In the summer months the tourists would drive up and park over across the heather-strewn tor, watching the prison through binoculars, getting turned on, I suppose, by the thought of all the evil men banged up inside. Funny that us cons were such an attraction – from a distance. If only some of them thought to come in and give a con a visit – just as Malcolm had come to see me. That might make a difference.

One day, dreaming away, I stayed too long up the ladder. Trevor didn't mind, but a passing principal officer did. My job was then to hold it steady at the bottom. Trevor did the climbing. The ladder caused quite a few problems actually. Normally after a job I would just lower it myself, shoulder it up and, with Trevor 'supervising' alongside, jog off to the next tower. Security risk, said the PO. You both have to carry it. Fine. Trevor goes in front to lead the way, I wag around behind like the tail on a border collie.

Security risk, said the PO.

Trevor might find himself with a sudden blinding headache, courtesy of me, and wake up to find the ladder propped up against the wall and his co-worker speedily on the trot down some green and pleasant valley.

Greenaway must go in front. That way he can be kept an eye on. So on round the nick we go sounding like something out of the Oxford and Cambridge boat race with Trevor bawling out commands from the rear to his team up front. All of them being me.

Talk about entertainment. Don't bend my ear about Laurel and Hardy.

Soon, however, the electrical 'team' had graduated to the big time: re-wiring. And not in the minor league either. A whole block we had to do. Round we went cell after cell, ripping down all the old iron pipe conduits, pulling out the rubbery black cabling, perished and flaky like charcoal in your hands, and sliding up the modern plastic-coated wiring through the new, tough, tamper-proof ducts.

Then was the time I would preach. To Trevor, when no one else would listen.

Day after day, as we worked together on the winter job of the wing, I told him the gospel. I repeated what had happened to me, what God had done, what he could do for Trevor if only he would let him, and so on.

He listened, sometimes patiently, sometimes with ridicule, often with complaint — but nothing came of it. A bit of a soft kid by my reckoning. He had always been proud to have the 'hard nutter' gang president around — and used to question me long and regular about the bundles and the bikes and the birds. But turn Christian? That he couldn't handle.

But he stuck with me — he was doing his duty. If he

had a Jesus-freak on his hands — well, it was better than a junk-freak or a nonce. Getting into Jesus didn't seem to matter much either way. Until, that is, his wife was expecting their first child. He met me at the entrance of H wing one morning and I didn't need a degree in trick-cycling to see he was a worried man.

"What's up, Mr James?" I opened, careful-like. His private life was no concern of mine unless he chose to make it so.

"It's Janet, she's sick, the baby's due in eight weeks, but she started bleeding last night, you know. . . " He looked away, half in anguish, half in embarrassment.

"The doctor came first thing, told her to go to bed and rest. But you see she's lost three babies already. . . they just, well, they just miscarried. I just don't know what we'll do if this one. . ."

He tailed off, a miserable, ashen figure, his brown trade coat over his prison officers' working uniform flapping open unheeded in the biting cold wind.

He was confused and deeply worried. He wasn't a strong man, and I could see that this was hitting him hard. It was so unexpected, now so near to the birth — and on top of three disappointments, three deaths, already.

"She'll be all right," I said gently and, unlocking the door to the wing with his keys, I led him inside to where we'd left off work the day before. "I'm sure she will."

Thankfully, so thankfully, I didn't right away rush in and preach at him, or talk of his sins, or remind him of his need of God and salvation or whatever, just then. What he needed was a loving hand and a word of human comfort. God held my tongue.

It turned into a quiet day.

But towards the end of it I did seem to feel the pressure of the Holy Spirit building up inside me, telling me that I should say something about my faith, even so.

I waited for the right moment to catch him.

"Trevor, I think I should pray for your wife – I mean really pray. You see, I know God will help her out. He will, I know it."

He nodded. "Yes, Brian, of course. You do that. Thanks."

But I kept my word. In among my many, often wild and desperate prayers bent over the bunk in my peter each night, with *lights. . . out!* echoing up and down the landings, I offered up Trevor's wife, and her baby, for healing before my God.

I asked for a miracle – the doctor had later confirmed it was almost certain the baby was about to abort. His wife had been moved to hospital. Trevor took compassionate leave. I was taken off the electrical job and moved back to work with the rest of the maintenance party – I couldn't be allowed to work alone without formal supervision.

Nightly I continued my appeal to God.

Nearly a week later I was told I had my old job back. I met Trevor in the usual place outside H block.

"Brian!" He smiled and slapped my shoulder. "It's stopped. The bleeding's stopped! They're keeping her in of course, for tests and everything, *but it's stopped!* It just happened. Just happened."

Not long after I had to join up with the rest of the maintenance party again. Trevor was again on compassionate leave.

He had become a father.

10

FREE!

I hope you don't mind me writing to you, as I have not got a family who I can write to. . .
John, HMP Dartmoor,
long-term-'solitary' at the time of writing.

Getting a letter comes second only to a visit in the league of hopes for the average con.

Trouble was the average con − certainly in the Moor − didn't have an awful lot of people keen on either visiting him or doing any writing.

Some had family. To start with. They would get letters on and off pretty regular. But as the bird went on these would tail off. Somebody said once that absence makes the heart grow fonder. But when the absence is due to being a criminal banged up facing much over five years' bird, then not only do hearts grow cooler, they clear off altogether.

Most in for five or more years lose everything.

Wife, kids, family, mates, house and home. The lot. There is nothing doing for them on the out at all.

Unfortunately a con can't just fade away like his memory. Some wish they could. Sharp objects are banned in cells for more than one reason. No, he must live and work and eat and sleep − and dream of the day when his bird will be over and he can get out and start again.

But there will be no one there. Why should there be?

Five, ten, fifteen years is a long time for a wife to cuddle a photograph, a brother to defend the name of a man behind bars, a landlord to remember who once paid the rent.

Time enough, though, for 'uncle' to become 'daddy' to a daughter, for drinking mates to recall a different 'all-time winner' in pub darts, for someone banged up for the greater part of his daily life in cell 38, E Wing, HMP Dartmoor to become, incredibly, a man of 'no fixed abode'.

A drink to 'absent friends' gone absent. Now someone else is buying his round.

I was lucky, I had been leader of a big gang of mates. Sure, some had shopped me up, but some still stayed loyal. I got a letter about once every two months.

It usually wasn't from them.

The mail call was a high point of the day. The screw would come out with a bundle of letters in his hands and stop on the bridge across the landings. Standing there he could look down the whole line of cells on both sides of the wing.

We'd all be getting our eating irons out for lunch, washing after work, waiting in our peters, and he would begin shouting out the names:

"Andrews, Hayman, Taggart, Jensen, O'Connor. . . " The litany would ring round the high, echoing building. And all would grow quiet, ears pricking up, hoping, praying for a name to be included. If it was, a face would appear along the landing. A hurried wipe of the mouth with a grey sleeve, a half-doubting, half-believing glance across at the bridge and then a clatter of footsteps down the steel ladder to beg at the hand of the chanting ringmaster. A grasp at the envelope, quickly, firmly, owning it, and then retreat to the welcome intimacy of the cell.

You've heard of 'more haste less speed'? That was how you went. Flat out, but playing it cool, nonchalant like. Nothing special, a letter. Hard cons don't run.

Big boys don't cry either.

Two or three come up at a time and the centre-piece of this little performance, gradually reducing his handful of paper, sings on. Calling the tune.

"Harrison, Wills, Doughman, Seddon, Sharp, Collins. . ."

Gradually hope fades. The clatter and chatter returns, more softly, to the wing. The show is over for the day. The screw leaves his stand on the bridge. He doesn't bow.

Getting a letter can mean everything.

Of course what it said might just mean everything too.

All cons steeled themselves as much as they could for the 'dear John' letter. The trouble was there was usually no warning of the crash. It came as the usual letter from the wife or girlfriend, desperately awaited perhaps, especially as they had been coming less frequently lately, and getting shorter. . .

It was a long one. Surprise and delight. A real, long letter from the heart.

It was that all right. Straight from the heart:

"I had. . . been meaning to tell you. . . so lonely here on my own. . . someone to play with the kids. . . got fed up stopping in all the time. He's taking care of me like you couldn't. He keeps me warm at nights. He takes me out in his car. Buys clothes for your kids. Sorry, I couldn't take it alone anymore, sorry if this hurts a bit, sorry, sorry, sorry. The kids send their love. Sorry. . ."

I've seen the hardest cons crack up and freeze for days on end after a 'dear John' letter.

Understandable, of course. Society's offenders, consequences of punishment, and all that.

They're people. And, as I was beginning to understand, people Jesus Christ died for. He died with a con on either side, and he spoke to them both – one understood, one didn't – but he spoke to them even while he was dying. He loved the cons.

Not very grand for a King. But that was the way God had it planned.

He knew who needed Jesus: those who knew they had failed.

"I've not come to save the 'good'," he said. "But the bad and the ugly."

Put it another way: "I have not come to call the righteous to repent, but sinners – it is the man who is sick who needs the doctor." You can see why I got hooked on my Bible.

Christ 'sets the prisoner free'. Another text. Loads of characters get put inside in the Bible. There are some strange escapes too.

Of course the message is often about the prisoner shut up in sin, self-centredness; the prisoner to sex, to money, to ambition, to Satan, all of these. True, but not just that. He sets the prisoner of society free too. The stabber, the rapist, the thief, the fraud – all have been released by the love of Christ.

He still loves cons – completely. Why or how I don't know. God knows, I'm unlovely enough – but he broke through to me.

But still, Christian or not, I stayed banged up, inside the Moor. About two years on I got a letter. A 'stiff' letter: sent to me illegally, not passed through the prison system and censored. It was from Pete the

Animal, still doing his bird in Winchester. He had slipped it to a con being moved on down to the Moor. I could see when I opened it that it had been written in desperation and misery — in a hurry too, I thought. Probably tried to get all the details down before the transfer day — to make sure that I got it delivered, personally.

I sat unsteadily on my bunk, the cheap notepaper crackling in my hands, reading the tortured message written by my lieutenant — he hoping that somehow, by sharing with me the horrible burden he bore, it would lift from his own shoulders.

It wasn't pleasant. Six of my mates, men of my chapter, had overdosed on drugs, in one week. All had died.

As far as I could tell from the unhappy scrawl none of them had intended to make that trip their last. Maybe it was mixed dope, bad acid. Who knew? Who cared?

By the end of the page I was smearing the straggling lines with my tears. In the end I had to stop reading. The story told, Pete had then gone on with a series of anguished cries for help and understanding to his one-time leader and friend. I could see him banged up in Winchester, poor Pete, hearing the horror story through the grapevine, knowing that the only thing he could do was somehow get word to me.

But the tears weren't for him, nor even were they simply for the death of my friends. They were tears of frustration that I had not been able to get out to them in time to tell them about Jesus. Heartless? Why? Jesus meant everything to me now — and still he does. He had turned me from a violent, no-hope junkie into a person again.

Alone in my cell — and with the help of his servants — people like Malcolm Goodman, new Chaplain Noel

Proctor and others, he had completely changed me. He made me see that life is not only about what you can see and hear, but that there is a whole world of the spirit — which is every bit as important.

What can be more important than facing eternity?

Hell on earth I knew something about, but I had become convinced that a far more real hell faced those who did not know and could not claim the safety of Jesus, had not learned that Jesus had died for them and their sins.

The Bible makes it perfectly clear. It isn't nice, but it's there. And, as I say, you read the whole book or none at all. My six riders of the road, friends, followers, mates had gone to their deaths knowing nothing of Jesus Christ and the hope he offers. I had not been able to tell them. I had not been free to do so.

Gradually my tears of sorrow and helplessness turned to rage. Letting the letter fall to the cold floor unheeded I looked up at the small square of light, my only contact with the outside world. The small ventilator square through which my pet budgie — now long since replaced — had flown out into the winter night to die on the Moor, the square barred by stout iron. I grabbed up at the bars, wrenching uselessly with both hands.

"Isn't it enough, Lord?" I cried. Tears streaming once again down my face.

"They hadn't a hope, Lord. No hope at all." I twisted at the grating in an agony of emotion.

"Who will tell people like that? No one cares for them. Lord, you must let me out. *Let me out!*" I cried out, choking.

"They know me, they will trust me. They will listen. I know what it is like!" Pain shot through my hands.

Gradually my anger subsided. My tears dried salty on my lips. I sank to the floor, exhausted.

A few weeks later I was called in to see the deputy governor — at 'requestmen and defaulters'. I stood again at the end of the long table.

"Greenaway 278431, sir."

"Greenaway. I don't have to tell you that we are all very surprised at the change of attitude and, well, er, general improvement we have noticed in you over these past few months.

"I understand that it has something to do with a new-found conviction in the church. . . "

He paused. I nearly opened my mouth to put him straight on that one — it was Jesus, not the 'church', that had made the difference, such as it was. But this guy was winding up to something important. I didn't want to stop his train of thought — it was rattling fast in my direction.

"Hmm, well, whatever it is seems to be working and we have decided as a consequence to advance your date for Parole Board."

He mentioned a date, less than a month away.

I rocked on my heels. Parole? In the Moor only about two people a year get parole — and certainly not GBH merchants. Violent types had to do their full bird.

I gulped out a reply and was marched out, my head spinning.

The next month was the longest ever, and you can bet I was a model prisoner. Whatever God had done in my life I tried to improve on. I worked hard and smiled at everyone, helped people out, gave away snout — and generally made myself thoroughly sickening. But it made no difference. The Parole Board would be looking at my record over the year, not at my schoolboy behaviour over the last couple of weeks.

The Board was a moving experience: mostly in my stomach.

It was formed of a panel of local people of quality. Respectable and safety-conscious types. Good citizens. They weren't about to unleash a violent con on society, however often he smiled and sang songs about Jesus.

They grilled me for over an hour. I was told to wait outside.

After a few minutes of discussion they called me back inside. An elegant lady spoke, with a posh accent and a voice that could stop a bus at two hundred yards. She was summing up. Everything was dressed up with conditions and reflections and considerations and a lot of other things.

Finally she got to the punchline.

"After a most careful analysis of your prison record, and detailed consultation and examination of all the pertinent circumstances, my colleagues and I have decided to recommend you for parole. . . "

I beamed out idiotically all over my face. I was turned about and marched out.

Over the moon and treading mainly on air, I followed the screw down the passageway of the admin block and out into the open exercise yard.

The Dartmoor air smelt different; the wall, the wire, the dogs, the towers, hardly existed. I felt as though I could walk on for ever.

"I've done it," I sang to myself. "I've done it. I've got parole!" I nearly shouted it out across the yard. A number of faces were turned enquiringly in my direction. Everyone knew where I had just come from. Was it a 'knock back', or was it parole?

As the words were on my lips, it seemed as though a small voice in my heart quietly but firmly spoke in contradiction.

"No, Brian, *you* have done nothing."

When I eventually spoke, the words came out

differently, the enquiring faces around me were impressed and disbelieving at the same time.

"Yes, I've got parole. But it wasn't down to me. You see — it's *Jesus* who sets the prisoner free. . . "

A few weeks later he did.

11

OUTSIDE THE WALL

Remember Jesus Christ, risen from the dead, descended from David, as preached in my gospel, the gospel for which I am suffering and wearing fetters like a criminal. But the word of God is not fettered. . .

Paul, HM (Imperial) Prison Rome,
beheaded about AD67

The phone was ringing.

It often does in our little South London home. Most things start with a call on the phone. Or a letter.

When I left the Moor I was let out on conditional probation – the condition being that I spent most of the time at a drug rehabilitation centre. This was to let me down lightly. For who knew what cravings would boil to the surface now I was free at last, outside the wall.

At the centre, I learned to relate to real people again, adjusting now as a Christian, from the distorted world of cons and curses to something more sane and sure.

But strangely, as I stayed there, and later when my time was up and I really went 'outside', I felt more and more strongly that the fearful and shadowy world I had left behind actually held the key for me. The key to my future as well as the record of my violent past.

It was obvious to me from the start that cons needed the light of Christ in a big way, and that God was always trying to reach out to unhappy, screwed-up people like

me and my old mates. The desperate urge to talk about
Jesus to my biking mates also left me with the feeling
that I ought to be talking to cons inside. A lot were cons
now anyway.

But I fought that feeling, hard. I didn't want to hear.

"Lord, I just want to be *me*, now," I protested. "Just
normal-like. All I need now is to be ordinary, that's all,
nothing fancy. Good citizen Greenaway. Talk about
Jesus to my old mates, quiet-like. Get to church on
time, that sort of thing."

The trouble with God sometimes is that he doesn't let
up. All the while I was making my objections, I could
hear this other voice, quietly underneath.

"Yes, Brian, you *have* been there, and because of that
you can talk to them. You understand their ways, how
they think and feel — how they hurt. When you speak
they will know you understand what it is to sink so low,
get bitter — be condemned. I need you. You can be a
bridge between us."

Did I say I heard it? Well, maybe not, but it was there
anyway. My new master was putting out a call, no
question, and I could see answering it was going to be a
lot tougher than burning down lanes on my mean
machine. It would be a harder fight — in terms of time,
spiritual (and physical) danger, and sheer slog — than
any bundle I had led in gangland.

Could I take it on?

But I already knew the answer. To my mind I had no
choice. I had already received so much.

I went along to a Bible College, as I needed badly to
get some real light on God's ways of dealing with
people. I gave out a few flashes of my own — to some of
the others there, I might add. But I was taught to think
and to question, and to begin to understand some of
God's words in the Bible. It was an important time. My

language also improved.

I also fell in love with Claire, a student teacher, who then decided to take me on for keeps, and marry me – we now have three children. And I went to work with the London City Mission, a team of missioners reaching out to London's urban working-class. At first this took me to dockland Isle of Dogs. But two years later I moved to work in prisons – in London and often further afield.

In fact, though, my work comes to much more than that. The pimps, drug-pushers, prostitutes, down-and-outs and the rest are all either heading into prison or heading out – and they too need God's message.

What sort of problems? Let me tell you about just some of my recent cases. Not the pick of the bunch. Just some out of many. No, I'm sorry, not cases: people. People who have been put in touch with me for help.

12

RESCUE

On quite a few occasions your name has been mentioned so I've decided to write a letter to invite you. . .

Les, HMP Grendon, short-term

The phone was ringing insistently in the downstairs room I call my 'office' at home, drowning out the chirp and chatter from my cage of (Zebra) finches, a reminder of the days when a bird was my only companion.

With difficulty I finished off the sentence I was typing – a letter to a con at Strangeways – switched off the answering machine and took the call myself. Should have left it on the tape; impatient, that's me.

"Brian?" I recognized the voice of a London City Missioner. He was trying to decide whether he was speaking to a machine or me.

"Yes, it's me, Jim," I confirmed.

"Sorry to trouble you Brian. . . " he began. (Well, it showed he was a thoughtful man – or else there was real trouble in the pipeline.)". . . but there's this girl. She's a pro in Soho, hooked on 'H', and just become a Christian. She badly needs somewhere to go, Brian, and I thought you might know a place?"

"Jim, I dunno. . . how much heroin is she shooting?"

"Nearly £200 a day, I'm afraid. Her pimp keeps her stuck on it to keep her working. I've just got to get her away. She has made a real commitment to Jesus, Brian, but the 'H' has got its hooks in − deep − and so has her minder. He follows her everywhere. Is there nowhere, Brian?"

I talked to him some more.

Her story was by no means unusual. She had come to London (from Glasgow) believing there would be work, and found nothing. When she ran out of money she began to walk the streets and had met a few 'friends' − the only people who would speak to her it seemed − who had been pleased to help her 'get away from it all' with a gift or two of an innocent white powder. Grateful for their attention she tried it. It worked. She floated high for several days on what they had given.

Casually they had gone on to suggest there was one way of working which would help them all afford to 'relax' more often. Shocked and frightened at first, but desperate for companionship − and money − she had gone to work on the streets. Soon, as a prostitute, she found she could earn a lot of money. She also found she spent it.

Her friends had explained that now, being so well-off, she should consider paying a 'reasonable price' for her relaxing trips. These were actually needing more and more of the herion, for that was what it was, to make them even half-comfortable. There were real bad trips too, which had to be made up for. The price rose. Soon she was earning − and spending − nearly £200 a day, all on H. Her home was a sleazy flat in Soho, run by her pimp. She slept days and worked nights along with other girls. She mainlined now, jabbing herself, much more of the time.

Then, by some miracle she had gone along to a

Christian meeting. The words spoken had hit home. She had realized her desperate need of Jesus and had accepted him as her only life-saver, her only hope, in her deadly circumstances.

She had also found she was pregnant with twins.

I put down the phone and sank to my knees. What could I do? There were so few drug-centres, so many addicts. No one would take her.

"Lord," I cried, "what should I do? What *can* I do?"

The door banged and Claire, my wife, came in with Emily close on her heels. Emily is the eldest of our three children, born shortly before we went to Bible College, eight years ago – two years after I walked out of the Moor with my ticket to freedom.

"Oh, Brian, can you see if . . . " She stopped suddenly seeing my face. "Brian . . . "

She knew the look immediately. It came when there had been a cry for help, a challenge that God had sent our way – something he seemed to be doing more and more these days.

Letters from cons (half a dozen a day), calls to take meetings (in and out of prison), calls for advice from churches asking how to help cons, or sometimes, sadly and bitterly, how to get rid of cons and ex-cons from their 'offended' congregations. Or, like now, our own home, our family haven, suddenly invaded by a nightmare story of tortured lives, horror and deprivation. Supper round the TV with the shadow of death – on the doorstep. It was nothing new and she said a silent prayer for strength before she continued.

"What is it?" she asked, gently. God had answered her prayer. Emily left us and went on into the kitchen.

I told her briefly and added that I didn't know what to do. I had ten letters to finish to cons, all urgent, a meeting to prepare and the church Bible study to go to that night. We prayed briefly together. She went to get some tea and I continued alone.

Shooting that much heroin the girl would be dead by Christmas and the children, if they lived, would be addicts from birth.

I knew I had to try. I turned back to the phone.

I dialled every 're-hab' centre in London and the home counties.

I got tired of hearing my own voice:

"Oh, ah, hello, my name is Brian Greenaway. I'm attached to the London City Mission . . . mm, yes, that's right, well I'm calling urgently because I have just heard of a very serious case of drug dependency, it's . . . ah, no room at present? A long waiting-list? Right, I understand, sorry to have troubled you, er . . . maybe you could think of somewhere else?"

Mostly there would be another idea, another number to ring. It helped when saying no to be able to offer something else — though it was normally done in the tone of voice you would expect to hear telling you that a good bet for a safe crossing of the Atlantic was the Titanic.

My mug of coffee was stone cold on the table and my pork chop a dried-up question-mark on the plate when I eventually got through to a centre on the south coast.

A man answered whose voice was familiar — but from where? I knew as soon as I said who I was. Bible College. We caught up with all the news and then I explained my call.

He was doubtful. I told him the tale of the past two hours. He relented.

"All right, Brian . . . for you."

I thanked him as though I'd just won a million and called Jim.

The next afternoon found me driving up Tower

Bridge Road to the Mission HQ, which is tucked away on the south bank of the River Thames between the famous bridge and the old wartime cruiser (now a museum), HMS Belfast. Building bridges, and fighting battles: just about right for a working Christian, eh?

After a brief word with Jim — and keeping a wary eye open for the girl's minder, whom he had been careful to 'lose' when bringing her to the HQ — we showed the unhappy lass down to the car and headed south out of town.

She was in a bad way. Facing cold turkey — as she knew she must — she had dosed herself up, which in real terms meant she wanted to throw up every five miles or so along the way. At a tap from Jim I would pull over onto the hard shoulder . . . I kept my eyes on the road; the sound effects were bad enough.

Eventually, late in the evening, we hit the coast and drove along to the centre and welcome. We left her with them, exhausted and shivering from the first effects of withdrawal.

In three days I was back again. She had threatened the staff with violence and had to be moved on — for the benefit of the other patients as well as the safety of the staff. My search started over.

This time I found a 'safe house' in North London for her. There she responded better — to treatment and love.

Not long after I found out that her mother was alive. She was well-off and living back in Scotland. A keen church-goer too. I was over the moon. Her mum, finding her lost daughter — and a new Christian as well; she would surely be overjoyed to have her back home and nurse her to health out of the shadow of the dreaded 'H'. She could afford the best of treatment for the kids too.

But I dreamed in vain. The mother refused to answer any of my calls and letters. She wasn't interested. Her own reputation perhaps was more important to her than the plight of her daughter. She could not admit to her 'decent' church friends that she had a prostitute daughter hooked on hard drugs.

Understandable really.

I wonder if God sees it that way. He hasn't given up on his new daughter.

After three moves of accommodation she eventually settled, though sadly she lost both babies before birth – the effect of the drug. It has been four months now. She is getting on top of the 'H' and has left the streets – and, most important of all, is turning more and more of her life over to her new manager: Jesus. Her faith and understanding are deepening all the time.

In my book, hers is a success story, thank God though she still has a long way to go.

13

POISON

*But I am no better off now so either I was fool enough
to think I was right in what I was doing and saying or
Satan had me believing everything was OK.*
   Phillip, Broadmoor Mental Hospital, life

I met Dan not long after he had come out of prison.
Once again it was through a contact in the London City
Mission. He seemed a nice enough lad – at first
anyway.

On the out he wanted to go straight. But he had a big
problem with drink. He was a chronic alcoholic. Even a
whiff of the stuff and he would go haywire. Normally he
used to start drinking to drown his sorrows and then, as
he became depressed, drank more to forget his deep
feelings of failure.

One day he was so low he had climbed up onto the
roof of a building to jump off and end it all.

Well, he jumped. But he tripped as he fell and hung
himself up by his trousers on the guttering.

This sad performance had been watched with
mounting alarm by a Christian couple who happened to
live in the flat below, and as he hung from their roof
screaming and cursing they managed to reach out and
catch hold of him, dragging him in through their
window.

Then they talked to him, first until he was sober and then until he had seen the state of his life and come to realize something of the mess he was making of it without God.

Shortly afterwards he told them he had become a Christian.

Not everybody was too sure, however. His drinking continued and now he protested that he needed to drink in order to cover his feelings of guilt — over letting God down by drinking.

It was pretty obvious that things weren't too straight in his mind at all, and it wasn't long before he tried to kill himself again — by drowning this time, rather than jumping off a roof.

But he had no more success in that either. He managed to detach himself from a London bridge, but was speedily dragged out of the water by the Thames river police who tend to keep an eye open for this sort of thing.

It was around about this time that I had a phone call from our local pastor explaining that Dan's wife, a very long-suffering Christian woman, was really under terrible pressure — due to all of this plus the fact that she had just discovered she was pregnant again. They already had two children.

I went round to their house. Dan was drunk. His greeting was shocking and shambolic. He lunged at me with a kitchen knife. I avoided the blow and turned him back into the house. His wife's pale face appeared in the doorway.

"Oh, Brian, thank God you've come," she whimpered, her voice drowned immediately by a roar from Dan who had twisted round and started up at me again with shouts and threats.

He was way over the top and knowing I had a history

of violence was perhaps trying to taunt me into killing him.

I calmed him down, slowly, dodging his wild blows and turning a deaf ear to his shouts. At last they both sat down with a cup of tea. Then I talked to them and ended up asking them round for Sunday lunch at our place. I hoped there, at least, we could have a go at sorting things out.

Next Sunday I dropped round to pick them all up. Dan refused to come. I protested, but he wouldn't budge. He was going to stay home. I was determined that at least his wife and kids should have a decent meal inside them and a chance to chat and play, so I made no more fuss. He seemed fairly sober.

"You're *sure* you'll be all right?" I queried.

He waved us away. Of course he would.

After lunch and tea, and a long talk with his very wound-up, but determined, wife I drove her and the children reluctantly back home.

There was no answer to my knock on the door. There was no answer to my call up the stairs when we let ourselves in. There was no answer anywhere.

Worried, I climbed the stairs and looked into the bedroom – and heaved a sigh of relief. Dan was in bed asleep. I shook him. Still nothing. He seemed to be out cold. Then I noticed a stain of blood on the bedcover. I pulled it back.

Two rusty Stanley blades slithered to the floor. I ripped the remaining cover back. Blood drenched the bed. His arms were a mass of cuts and scrapes. He had been slashing at himself with the razor-sharp knives. It was a horrific mess.

I bent over him. It looked as though this time he had succeeded in his aim.

Then he moaned. I was wrong, he was alive. And,

judging by the smell, afloat on a sea of spirits.

I looked again at his arms. The wounding was all superficial – there were about seventy or eighty cuts, but no torn veins. Had he, again, really tried to kill himself? Or was he all the time trying to attract attention? The only thing I knew was that I had to get him to a hospital and 'de-tox' unit fast to dry him out. Maybe when his head was clear – then I could talk some sense into him.

Making sure that his wife or children didn't see him before I'd bound up his arms and cleared the sheets off the bed, I dragged him, deadweight, out to the car.

We got to the hospital. By then he had come round and begun to act wild. Dragging him behind me like a badly hooked-up articulated lorry – I went up to the reception desk and started to explain to the nurse on duty. But Dan was having none of it, slavering and cursing all over – and real angry. I was making my third attempt at explanation when who should walk into the reception area but a police sergeant on official business. Spotting him, Dan, as an ex-con, began to make generally known his strong views on the law in general, and the police in particular – all this as loudly as possible around the hospital foyer.

I grabbed his belt and, discovering from the nurse that the de-tox unit was over in a separate building, dragged him backwards through the automatic doors and across the courtyard. The sergeant, wise and helpful man that he was, saw and heard nothing.

But Dan was determined to make his visit memorable.

When we finally found the unit waiting-room he immediately leaped up onto the table in the middle, dancing up and down, old magazines and AA (alcoholics anonymous) literature scattering on the floor like overweight confetti — and daring me to do something about it.

I was just about to break a long-standing personal resolution and lay him out cold when the doctor came in to ask what all the noise was about. He saw the problem — dancing on the table — and ordered him out straightaway. I grabbed the doctor's arm and pleaded with him. Could he run a de-tox on him, please?

"Only if he is sober and willing for treatment," was his firm reply. "Until he is, get him out of here."

Hoping that Dan was happy, at least for the moment, I walked the doctor into the next room and explained the circumstances — Dan's waiting family, his attempts at suicide, and so on. Eventually he came round. "OK," he said, "I'll see what I can do."

Just then there came an almighty crash from next door. The two of us rushed through just in time to see the remains of the picture window splintering round Dan's feet. He had put his head through it. In his hand was a shard of glass, held like a dagger.

"Now I'll show you," he roared. I got to him just before he drew it across his throat.

The doctor kept his word and gave him the de-tox treatment.

Three weeks later he was dead drunk again.

He threatened his wife, and the local minister who had visited (the pastor who called me in the first place). The police were called and he ended up in Brixton Prison on remand. I visited him there. Within days I had another phone call from his wife.

"Dan set fire to the mattress in his cell," she wept, her voice strained and broken on the crackling line. "He's had to have surgery on both legs for the burns and they say he'll need skin grafting."

I said what I could, which wasn't much. She, saintly,

still accepted that this man was her husband. She knew that God would keep her throughout. All I could do was encourage her to hold on to that.

He has now been released, de-toxed again, and is living in London – apart from her, for safety's sake.

To me he seems an accident going somewhere to happen. I know that God *can* do something with him if Dan himself really wants him to. But he trusts his drink, the certainty of oblivion, more than the helping hand of God. And God will force no one against their will.

I am very much afraid that one day he will manage to kill himself with one of his attention-getting stunts – if that is what they are. The terrible thing is that there are people who do love him and care for him – more perhaps than he deserves. His wife, the church pastor – and Jesus himself.

But then none of us deserves the love of God. We have all messed up somewhere along the line. Don't I know it. But in that love there is forgiveness, if only Dan could see that.

I feel I ought to be able to do more for him. But he is not the only one. There are many more. My own time is limited; I must share it out.

With Dan I do feel I have failed.

But I pray. God can work even when I cannot.

14

GERRY

Greetings Brian and God bless you for your letter.
When I got your letter I was feeling very low and
depressed. . . thank you for your words of comfort. . .
I am very, very grateful and much better for
them. . .

Gerry, HMP Wakefield, nine years.

I have never met Gerry.

He is just one of the many hundreds of prisoners who
write to me week in and week out from over half the
prisons in the country. Each has his own tale to tell,
and I know each one.

Through their letters they tell me how they feel, what
they want, what they have or have not done to deserve
their bird, who they want me to see on the out for them,
if I can, and so on. All the letters are from unhappy
people, and the weight can get a bit heavy at times. But
I write back as best I can and leave the burdens that I
cannot handle for God to look after. It is the only way.

Gerry comes to mind because he has just had a knock
back. He'd been making an appeal against his sentence.
His stretch is nine years, when his sort of crime usually
carries around five. But his was a sex crime. Weighted
against him already, in a way.

He wasn't allowed to attend the hearing. Nor was the
solicitor I'd managed to put him in touch with, who was

hoping to defend the case. And the news just in is that the sentence stands.

I happen to think he is innocent – he's got me 'conned', as they say inside – which thing, let me tell you, doesn't happen very often. His prison chaplain happens to think so as well, and we've both been around prisons for a while. But whatever, the court thinks different and he's now facing the full nine years.

Most of it, of course, will be on his own. Being a sex case he is down to Rule 43 straight off. Banged up solo for maybe most of the day for his own safety. Gives you a lot of time to read and write.

That was where I came in. It was the chaplain at Brixton Prison who got hold of me first.

"Brian, I wonder if you could spare a few moments to write to this Gerry fellow?" he asked me, as we were chatting about some of the day's visits over a cup of tea in the canteen.

" . . . seeing as how I've got nothing better to do!" I laughed, finishing off for him.

My routine letter-writing to cons had already reached half a dozen a day. I could do without adding to the list just for the sake of it. I told him so.

"Well, OK Brian. But this chap told me that he had just read your book (*Hell's Angel*) and really got something out of it. He's a soldier, or was, quite a young lad really . . . " he went on, as though musing on some passing thought.

Well, he'd got me sown up tight at that. This con was obviously some tasty guy – a nutter who'd got out of line somewhere. A soldier is a fighter – and the chaplain knew I couldn't refuse the man he was describing, even with my present case-load. Talk about con artists. Some of these chaplains need a good talking to, I reckon.

The end of it was I ripped off a letter to this Gerry saying I'd heard about him. Did I know any of his friends on the inside (if he had any)? I mentioned the book and the chaplain and so on — the regular sort of chat I get into when I write a letter for openers.

I got back a bit of a blockbuster. Not only was the letter neatly written — the scrawl I have to work through from some cons even makes *my* writing look good — but it was thoughtful and open. There was just so much he had to say and questions he had to ask. Wow. There was no stopping the man:

"Firstly, thank you for your letter . . . it certainly lifted my spirits. There are so many things I want to say but it's hard to do that on paper, I feel that you know and understand though. Many things trouble me, my friend, some so much that I find myself unable to cope. So many changes sometimes. Does that make sense to you, Brian? You said that Jesus helped you to put your life right. How did it happen, Brian, how . . . "

And a lot more besides.

I banged back a reply and soon we had letters piling up each way. One of the things he mentioned a lot was his mum, and so did someone else I got in touch with who knew Gerry. I got the feeling that she was really doing everything possible to support him — and to fight his case for him on the out. So I decided to pay her a visit and give her some encouragement — and tell her I was getting on well with her son.

Well, I turned up at their home not long after and got a bit more of a surprise. It was a real neat place. Not rich, but nice and decent and well-kept.

There was I thinking I'd be running into the sort of place, well, you know — I've seen so many in this line of work — home all shot to pieces, that sort of thing. No, these people had kept their self-respect.

It was a bit of an odd meeting. Talking to his mother and her brother who also turned up, a pretty front-room, with tea and cakes and talking about their lad who had done so well in the army (smart photo on the sideboard), just left the service, did local voluntary work with the Samaritans, and so on. And all the while he's banged up in solitary on Rule 43 with nine years to run.

We got round soon enough to talking about life inside, though. And I told them about my time in particular, my meeting with God and the difference it had made. They both began nodding and agreeing in a strange sort of way. You get to expect a certain sort of reaction but theirs was different.

I asked them what they meant by it and both of them confessed that they were practising spiritists. It turned out that they were aware of the Christian message but were simply not able to accept it because of all their other convictions getting in the way.

Now I am quite convinced that the devil uses spiritists, often without them knowing or understanding quite what they've got into. The spiritual world is real all right, but not in the way they think. You see, the mystic world of the spiritist is no stranger to prison. The con is in a mess − by definition − and every one of them is looking for meaning, and power. The practice − and often the porn − of mystic or 'spiritual' arts is one attractive route to this power.

Black magic, seances, ugly visitations and foul books are all part of prison life. Some are into it really deep. One of the alternative, and quite common, uses of the dark beeswax used in sowing mailbags is to make 'satan dips' − black candle strips for the celebration of black mass in someone's peter or other dark corner during association hour.

But Gerry's mother was spiritually confused. This only gave the lie to all that the spiritists believed and held. Her convictions were of no help at all to her son and of no comfort to herself in her distress. There was no one waiting to give help or comfort on 'the other side', no one there with a vital message for her that would make everything clear and the whole terrible episode comprehensible. There was nothing – except, maybe, the unheard, taunting laughter of the father of lies.

I don't know, of course, but it may well be that the whole of Gerry's miserable fate is down to his parents' interest in these spirits. Once you let the devil in he brings destruction. Nothing else. Maybe he'd been given enough influence in that family to take a young life and arrange the circumstances of its collapse. From what I know I don't think Gerry is a sex case. But the evidence certainly makes him look like one.

I don't reckon to put myself up with the apostle Paul, but, like him, I'm not completely ignorant of Satan's dirty tricks. I've seen them knocking about too often. And this one makes all the right noises. His family, so sophisticated, had been messing with spiritual dynamite, and it was child's play to make it blow up in their faces.

I left their home with a deep admiration for the love of his mother and the lengths she had gone to try and get him released. She had testimonies and depositions, great heaps of letters and documents attesting to his movements and other details at the time of the crime. It must have taken many long hours of painstaking work to get together.

But I also left with a deep sense of regret. Even with this deep failure to contend with, they were not prepared to consider the one true and ready help in time of trouble – Jesus Christ. But there is hope. Since then she has come to several Christian meetings, I hear. She is looking, for sure.

Gerry's moments with the spiritual had not always been occult. In a moving letter to me, written in December, he recalled one of the many Christmases he had spent in Ulster as a soldier.

It was Christmas Eve. He and his patrol had been out at a road-bridge checkpoint. It was, as always, a nervy business. Part of the patrol crouched by the parapet, backs to the stone, rifles up at the ready, thumbs on the safety-catch, heads always turning and eyes darting around, watching for an unusual move, a sudden motion – the only warning of a violent attack. The others were out in the open, exposed, waving the cars to a halt, searching through the luggage, tense for a discovery that might end in a hail of bullets. The traffic piling up with late Christmas shopping, tempers were starting to rise.

It was an unhappy business. The afternoon was cold and night was falling – with the added danger that always brought.

Then suddenly, in one of the queueing cars someone started singing. Just a few lines of a Christmas carol. Another joined in and soon the whole bleak scene rejoiced to the chorus of 'Hark the Herald Angels Sing' and 'O Come All Ye Faithful'. The soldiers, infected by the spirit of the moment, joined in. Hands relaxed on pistol grips and metal detectors to tap in time with the music.

For a moment, Gerry felt, there was no more 'them and us' – just the rightness of it all, the sense of peace and calm, so different from the tension of the day, so unwordly and apart. A peace that passed all understanding, that spoke to him of Someone greater.

He has never forgotten that moment. He made that clear in his, almost poetic, writing as he struggled to grapple with his new circumstances that first Christmas on the inside.

We continued writing. I did my best to answer his questions — an ever-mounting stream, about God, Jesus and the Bible. I had to fall back on good old Mrs Wilmer's teaching more than once. Take this for example:

"Brian, when Christ called out to his father: 'My God, my God why has thou forsaken me?' What was he saying? I have thought about it so much . . . could you please explain it to me?"

I have gone into the green, tin filing-cabinet where I keep all my letters and replies, and here is what — with God's help — I sent back:

"Gerry . . . to answer your question: Had God deserted Jesus? No. He was following in God's path. In his agony 'My God' is an affirmation of his faith. But Jesus is suffering something he has never known — the experience of abandonment by God. He had been betrayed, mocked and beaten all but to death — but it was a far deeper spiritual agony he suffered, alone with God's anger, and wrath fell on him *for our sakes*. That meant that all the unclouded communion he had known with his father was broken, as he took on himself all the sin of the world — past, present and future. He bore our sin (Hebrews 9:28) and bore the curse (Galatians 3:13) making a sin offering for *you* and me (2 Corinthians 5:21). The only barrier between God and man *ever* is sin, and in those three hours Jesus saw that barrier and felt it, so that all who believe in him would and could be saved (John 3:14-16). So, through your own question, I would challenge you my friend — what does this mean to you? It isn't rubbish because I have personally known the forgiveness for all I have done, and experience – now – a personal relationship with God through his son Jesus Christ."

Whew! Pretty good preach, huh? Well, I don't mess about if someone asks a question like that. I figure he wants to know the answer.

Gerry did. Not long after, I got this:

"You know, Brian, my friend, it all comes down to two words: Trust and Faith. How long have I suffered to find that simple truth out.

"I pray now that Christ Jesus will receive me and change me. I know that the Lord could say, 'I do not know you'. But although I fear that rejection I put my life into His hands. That is all I can do: Trust and have Faith."

"Well, Brian, I have stepped off . . . I am at his mercy . . . the Lord willing, I will not hit the ground."

Gerry didn't hit the ground. For, as with all who truly repent, Jesus came in and gently lifted him – alone, convicted, imprisoned – up to himself.

Now he has someone to share his cell.

15

IT'S COLD OUTSIDE

I'm down, I guess, because I feel I have been let down so much by those claiming to be Christians. I have grown wary and suspicious . . .
John, HMP Wandsworth, four years.

I would also like to tell you about Steve.

Steve is the first person I ever visited in a proper sense when I set up as a prison evangelist. Of course by then I knew a lot of cons, and had talked to quite a few about my faith. But Steve was my first official case.

I met him first in Wandsworth Prison and, following the visit, began to write, setting the pattern that now, five years on, has become the norm in my work with prisoners.

Before you jump on me, I don't go in just so as I can preach the gospel. That's pretty important to me, but unless these cons become real friends I don't feel I have the right to share anything at all with them. So it takes time and usually a number of letters — and visits, if these can be arranged — before I have the confidence to share honestly what I believe. I am pretty direct, though, and don't cover up if they ask right out. But unless they feel they are asking something of a friend, it just isn't sincere or worthwhile.

I remember the early visits. Often we would all roll up as a family, because that is what cons miss so much — the love of a family. Just to see a family sitting there can give them hope. Especially when the kids are just acting normal, smiling at people or messing around even. It is so open and honest; no hang-ups.

It was summer, and me not long out of Bible college, with Claire my wife and Emily, my eldest daughter — still, then, so young. We'd pitch up outside Wandsworth in the heat and dust of a hot London afternoon, waiting perhaps an hour or so with a crowd of other visitors for the porter's gate to swing open at visiting time. The air in the visiting room was always stifling with antiquated ventilation and thick with tobacco smoke. The visitors do their best to hide their nerves, or anger or pain, by smoking around three cigarettes at once.

Whilst we were waiting for the cons to be brought next door to meet us, the noise (above the coughing) was all blue abuse thrown at the screws by the visitors. They were trying to wind them, or chat them, up — turning on the aggro in any case. What a way for me to introduce my new, young family to the work which I felt God had called me to.

But Steve responded. He loved those visits and began to benefit from our prayers and those of others whom we knew. He was one of those who responded to my friendship and then later to my chat about Christian faith.

It turned out that he had been involved with something like this as a young lad. He had even had an experience of God at an early age, and grown up in a Christian home. (This isn't always the blessing it sounds. Sometimes although a true Christian home is the most wonderful thing on earth, it can leave you with weak defences.) In any case Steve had grown up and moved out of the influence of his parents and church, and one day he got so depressed about life that he set fire to the building in which he was living.

Now arson is a very serious offence. It is very close to murder, and in the experience of the police it very often turns out that way. If you set light to a building there is no knowing where it can end – or who might get trapped in it and burn.

So Steve was weighed off heavily. Seven years in fact. He made an appeal – against the length of sentence – and had it reduced to five.

He was moved to Parkhurst, which he found very tough. But even so he read some of the Christian paperbacks I sent him (how useful *they* are – inside you have so much time to read). Along with things I said and wrote to him, these brought him to recommit his life to Jesus Christ.

Sure he had a few problems. He had to work out whether he should be a Christian doormat or stand up for his rights – a hard balance to strike. But he seemed to be really growing in his faith, and he actually enrolled in a Bible correspondence course just like I had done in Dartmoor. He finished this and then went on to complete some studies that I had worked out myself specially for cons, called the Stepping Stones course. He was the first one. It is straight Bible teaching and, as the name says, it's supposed to help a con adjust and fit in – to the local church, the community, whatever.

Not long ago Steve finished his bird. His five years up, he walked outside a free man and was put up in a hostel just north of London.

Then the problems started.

When you're inside, you think that the Christian world outside is just waiting with open arms to welcome you when you get out. All these wonderful people longing to help you get back on your feet, ready with sympathetic advice and support.

You put up with the jibes of the cons, knowing that getting out is really worth looking forward to. Nothing else matters. Of course it does, really, but someone born again in prison is still a child in the faith, even if he has a lot of Bible knowledge inside his head.

But churches, and Christians, are often strange and alien to the believing con.

For a start he generally has no real skills for coping with the social side of the church life. Even just singing a new chorus or not sitting down at the end of prayer can be an acute embarrassment. Everyone else knows what to do and he doesn't. Sometimes the knife is twisted in the wound as his mistakes are highlighted by the church busybody (some of these can be about as graceful as an elephant with piles). And the ex-con starts wondering which Bible the church has been reading. 'Love your neighbour, return no man evil for evil, support the weak, encourage the fearful', says the Bible. But there doesn't seem to be a lot of it about in his neck of the woods.

So, while truly welcomed by some, he is very definitely a 'different sort of person' to most. Often he can see the change. He meets someone, makes a friend. Maybe, heaven forbid, even a girl. They're getting along fine, and he's invited back to the over-twenties fellowship after church on a Sunday. Next thing he notices is someone whispering to his friend in the corner.

He knows straight off what they are saying behind the mug of instant and the jaffa cakes. He doesn't need to lipread.

"I wonder if you had any idea that he's . . . you'd

never guess it would you?"

"I mean, I oughtn't to interfere, but did you realize . . ?"

"Mm, yes, five years is what I heard . . . "

He can kiss that friendship goodbye − at least in any genuine sense. They'll probably still talk to him, but only out of concern, or fascination. No more chance for a real friendship of equals. Of course any friendship is valuable, and people do need to know sometimes what a man has done. Also, by God's grace there are very lovely people in some churches. But in many there are not, and an ex-con is denied the right to be treated as a real person. He is not offered acceptance, that first crucial step out of the circle of crime and punishment.

So what happened to Steve?

This is just what happened to him. One day he got so depressed he set fire to the student hostel he was living in.

Now up for arson a second time, he has every chance of getting a sentence well into double figures.

How do I feel? Despairing, lost, angry at God for failing to stop him lighting the match? No. God doesn't work that way. We always have free choice, and he lets us choose. It's what makes us human. Nobody knows what sort of a personal fight Steve put up before he went his own way, denied his faith. More to the point, no one knows just how depressed he was − or how lonely he felt.

Rejected, by a thousand little slights. What last, seemingly minor thing took him the final step over the top? I haven't had a chance yet to find out.

But was there really no one he could turn to? Perhaps just no one near enough. I was on the end of a phone − or maybe I wasn't. Out, I guess, at the vital moment when he made the call − if he did. Perhaps I was listening to another's tale, or speaking at a meeting — maybe driving home from some distant prison. My answerphone, clicking its reply, would have been one more rejection.

I am hurt. Of course I am. I spent many hours at that man's bedside in his peter. I wrote dozens of letters to him and saw him take up again the faith I love so dearly, growing and flourishing as the Lord blessed him at my hands. The Bible studies, the prayer meetings — and the many times I spent with my family over the last six or seven years just lifting him up to Jesus Christ in prayer.

No, I never wanted to stamp him a success — a good bit of ministry. (Well done, Brian, you've saved another soul.) No way. I love him as a brother and I am hurt as a brother by what has happened.

And what about my little Emily? She has prayed for him ever since that first dusty, hot and rather frightening visit. She is older now, but I haven't had the heart to tell her, not yet. I must, of course, and I know God in his wisdom will choose just the right time for me to mention it. I hope she can understand, as much as anyone can understand. But it won't be easy. Not for any of us.

One thing Steve's story has done is to strengthen my conviction that the Stepping Stones idea simply doesn't go far enough. So far it has worked out as that little series of Bible studies which Steve took. But that isn't enough to help anyone in his position adjust to the demands — the really hectic demands — of life on the out.

Most of the cons walk out of the gates with the taunts of the screws at their backs:

"See you again soon. We'll keep your job for you,

don't worry. "Next time be sure and bring a friend."

It isn't very funny but it is true. Prison has become a familiar home where everything is done for you — not the way you'd like but at least it is done. Now the world waits for you to prove yourself. Not only are you back in the rat race, but now you're thrown back to try again, dragging the experience of prison along with you.

"Work? Sorry mate, can't take on old lags you know. Have to keep one eye on the till all day, wouldn't I now?"

"I don't let rooms to convicts, dearie. You'd sort of put off the proper clientele."

And the ex-con moves on as the pimps and the hookers knock after him and gain entry.

Of course it's his fault. He shouldn't have got bird. But he did and he can't just disappear.

The Stepping Stones Trust is something I have just set up with a group of friends to help some men to have a sort of semi-sheltered environment when they leave prison. There will only be a very few to start with, but it will help them to face the world outside again with some chance of success. We have received a grant and, along with another Christian trust, we are soon going to start building a hostel to house just eight ex-cons at a time, in bedsitters. They will have a Christian family as kind of houseparents, always on call, in a flat over the top.

It is a big step of faith for us, after so long working with the London City Mission. It's big too for everyone else involved, building a purpose-built hostel from the ground up. I've never done anything like it before — or even dreamed of it. But I know God is asking us to trust him to bring it all together and make it work. Over to you, Lord.

So far the plans have been drawn up and the plot of land secured in south-west London — on the site of the

Anchor Mission in Wandsworth. What a lovely name to greet a con when he strides up to the door and rings the bell! An anchor for him in the turmoil of sorting out his life. An anchor in the community for him to pause a while and get his bearings before setting sail on his own. The one completely secure anchor – Jesus Christ himself.

So far we have taken the first steps, in faith, believing as a family that this is the way he wants us to go forward in our ministry to prisoners. It is a heart-stopping adventure.

And even our brother Steve is not a lost man. Whatever has happened, whatever is about to, Jesus still loves him and so do many others. Next time – in ten, fifteen, twenty years from now when his bird is done – there will, by God's grace, be a stepping stone for him – one to tread on, not just read about. And he will find an anchor – maybe several – to hold him fast to his new life.

The praying – for him and for all of them – should be starting now.

16

CAN A PERSON CHANGE?

I am writing . . . to get as many churches, prayer groups, etc, praying for the church in Parkhurst — to be built up by the Holy Spirit. This is a very dark prison and we have a great need of prayer . . .
Jason, HMP Parkhurst, life

So you can see, my work now is dealing with people who are heading for prison, are inside, or have just left. Not just in London, but right across the country. People who have screwed up their lives so badly they have no one to turn to.

Usually, those that I meet have had some opportunity to give their lives over to Jesus — after all, I work with a Christian organization — but not always. I talk a lot in prisons to many hundreds who have never heard of him. And, even if they have, they don't understand what he has done — or what he can do if they will let go of that tight grip on themselves that insecure (and frightened) people so often have, and turn over fully to God.

So many — me included, sometimes — want to hold onto what we've got even if it is worthless. We know it, and it seems safer, however horrible and wrong.

That is what leads to terror and hopelessness. Only God can actually change human beings — really change them I mean. But, like any operation, surgery of the soul costs – and hurts.

From God's side the cost was his Son, Jesus. Hanging on a cross wasn't exactly the easy way home. But he went for it just the same, because his Father had told him it was the only way. He took him at his word. It cost – his life – but it worked.

We all, now, have a way through to God – by believing in Jesus. Don't ask me how it happens. I don't know. I don't know an awful lot of things. But I know it can turn your life around – the right way. And that's what matters.

Many cons I know, and visit regularly, have experienced such a change. It *is* real and lasting, though sometimes it's difficult for their friends and relatives to accept.

I remember Joe. He had become a Christian halfway through a spell inside, for violence and so on. He had been a Hells Angel like me.

He really came through to God and we had been writing a lot. Then the time came for his release and he got a shock. His wife blanked him completely.

She knew the sort of person he was, the sort of crimes he had committed and the sort of hardened criminal that he would be after seven years in a top-security prison. She wanted nothing more to do with him.

He wrote to me a broken man. He had just come outside, having experienced the most dramatic change in his life – and gone on to take all the stick for his Jesus-behaviour on the inside. And now his wife wouldn't see him, wouldn't even let him near the house. Could I do anything? He was going out of his mind not being able to see his kids and so on.

I shared all this with Claire and she decided to write

to his wife. She put in a copy of my other book *Hell's Angel*, which talks about the sort of person I was before I met Jesus, wrapped it up and sent it off.

We all waited anxiously for the reply. Back came a long letter, with loads of questions about me and my life and what was it like to be married to me, and so forth.

Claire answered them as fully and truthfully as she could, explaining about the 'old' and 'new' men that the apostle Paul talks about in the Bible and how Jesus had 'made all things new'. She wrote that provided I kept close to Jesus I wouldn't ever be going back to my old ways.

As a family we also prayed a lot for her, that she could really see and believe that this same sort of change can happen – and has actually done so in her husband.

Well, I don't know if it was Claire's letters or her reading my book through, but it wasn't long before we got another letter saying that she had decided to take her husband back 'for a trial period'. We knew that from her point of view this was a brave step. But we were sure of Joe and his faith.

As it turned out it was the sort of 'trial' Joe went for in a big way – which wasn't true of some of the others he'd been through.

Jesus has held them together ever since.

There are many stories like Joe's. There are many perverted, vicious men who have come through with Jesus to be reunited with their loved ones and families after many years apart. Some are still apart, separated by the glass partition of the visiting room, but have come together in other ways.

God is at work on the inside.

Even so, the first contact has to be made by people. I do what I can as I feel God has called me to work full-time in prisons, along with other groups like the Prison Christian Fellowship, the Christian Police Association and Prison Officers Christian Fellowship, the prison chaplaincy, visitors, and others. But it is never enough. Cons in and out of prison are people who need an awful lot of love and help – whatever crimes they have committed.

As Jesus said: "Whatever you do for these, the very least of my children, you do for me."

Perhaps you can write to a prisoner. Maybe you have some time to visit a prison near you and get to know one or two of the cons. Of course you may not be made welcome straight away. Cons are cynical, suspicious, hard – they've learned to be. Without Jesus they are only out for what they can get.

But they can change, and do. Often all it needs is a friendly face, and a word from God. All I had was just one visit and the gift of a Bible.

There was something else that meant a lot too: a helping hand when I got out. Someone to meet me and take me in while I got used to the real world again. It was vital.

Could you help a con in this way? Again it is a risk, we're not talking fairy tales; but maybe you could take on someone who has just left prison? Maybe someone whom you have come to know through letters and visits.

God promises to honour any who help others in his name. And he does.

Once, when I was visiting a small church to talk about prisons, a young couple came up to me after the meeting to ask if there was anything that they could do to help prisoners. The man explained he was a deacon of the church and wanted to lead the way by doing something practical.

At the time I had a man on my mind. He was doing 'double life', first in Wormwood Scrubs and later in Parkhurst, both maximum-security prisons. A murderer. He would never get out. I suggested they wrote to him.

They did write, and got replies. Later they made up their minds to visit. The husband went first. He went alone and, to be honest, a little fearful. Then they went as a couple. Finally the whole family, young children and all, rolled up at the prison one day.

The con was delighted — and so was the family. Now they exchange presents at Christmas and on birthdays and the family often makes extra 'holiday' trips to visit, plus of course everyone joins in answering his letters. Not with anything special — just ordinary personal news, difficult homework, loose teeth, life in the church, perhaps a Bible verse or two.

I met the deacon again the other day.

"You'll never know," he said to me, taking me to one side, "what a blessing that man has been to us. We really do love him now — every bit as much as one of the family."

Love. That about says it all, doesn't it?

As I have found for myself and other ex-cons are finding, God *is* love.

Hell's Angel

Brian Greenaway was president of a
Hell's Angel chapter. He was violent,
full of hate, deeply into drugs.

Then, in Dartmoor Prison, he had an
experience which changed him
completely.

This is Brian's own story – powerful,
sometimes ugly but real. It describes his
tough early years, his dramatic
conversion and his struggles to work out
a new way of life.

Worse Things Happen at Sea

'Nassau harbour, Paradise Bay. We
were steaming straight for the island. I
checked the compass and the line of
palms. About 600 yards to the shore.
   "Continuous soundings!"
   It was shoaling rapidly. Now or never.
   "Hard-a-port!"
   There was an anguished cough from
the wheelhouse − then silence.'

The ship may be bound for romantic
places, but for the navigating officer it is
no idyll. Comedy, love and near-disaster
form the happy blend which makes
these real-life stories an enjoyable read.
And the fact that this particular ship,
MV *Doulos*, is quite unlike any other.